THE
NEXT MILE℠
SHORT-TERM MISSIONS FOR THE LONG HAUL™

MILE POST DEVOTIONAL

Volume One

The Next Mile℠

Short-Term Missons for the Long Haul℠

MILE POST
DEVOTIONAL
Volume One

Authentic

Authentic

We welcome your comments and questions.
129 Mobilization Drive, Waynesboro, GA 30830 USA authentic@stl.org

and 9 Holdom Avenue, Bletchley, Milton Keynes, Bucks, MK1 1QR, UK
www.authenticbooks.com

If you would like a copy of our current catalog, contact us at:
1-8MORE-BOOKS
ordersusa@stl.org

The Next Mile^{SM}
Short-Term Missions for the Long Haul^{SM}

Leader Kit (includes one of each of the following)
ISBN: 1-932805-59-1

Leader Guide
ISBN: 1-932805-60-5

Goer Guide – All-Age Edition
ISBN: 1-932805-62-1

Goer Guide – Youth Edition
ISBN: 1-932805-61-3

Mile Post Devotional, Volume 1
ISBN: 1-932805-63-X

Roadmap
ISBN: 1-932805-64-8

Published in partnership with DELTA Ministries
PO Box 30029
Portland, OR 97294

Cover and interior design: Paul Lewis
Editorial team: Dianne Grudda, Sally Heerwagen, Ron Marrs, Shirley Radford,
Hilary Sarjent, Tom Richards, K.J. Larson

Printed in the United States of America

Foreword

As you return from serving in another culture for the first, second, or umpteenth time, you face the "re-entry process." Just because you may have done this before doesn't insulate you from the real-time effects of readjustment. You have experienced significantly different people and places, and *you have changed*. You will have a new appreciation for what God is doing in the world and how you "fit." Some of the cross-cultural relationships that you formed will influence you forever. It may take months for you to understand the total impact. You may even deny that you are different. However, after a period of time you will begin to realize and appreciate your changes in perspective toward the Lord and toward the peoples of the world he loves.

Your mission trip was only the first step in your journey. The second step begins as you choose to obey, grow, and get to know God as a friend, a loving Father, and most importantly as LORD. Our Lord wants to conform us to the image of Christ. To grow, you will need to exercise discipline. It will take effort on your part. Don't allow yourself to fall into old routines. As you mature, you will be able to understand God's will more clearly. The Word of God is the key to unlocking God's plan for your life. Don't misplace your key—choose to read and meditate on Scripture as you spend quality time with him.

The principles in this book will help you gain a wider view of the world from God's kingdom perspective. Each devotional will encourage and give valuable insight into living your life for Christ. May your excitement for Christ and your passion for reaching all people continue to grow as you seek to honor him.

Howard and Bonnie Lisech
Deeper Roots Publications
Orlando, Florida
www.DeeperRoots.com

WHO'S KIDDING WHO?
Andy Spohrer, WorldVenture

"Who's kidding who? Do those missionaries I just worked with *really* think they can make a difference and change those people? With all the poverty and religious opposition and so-o-o many people, it is really an impossible dream."

Do you sometimes have these thoughts? Sure, we all do if we are honest. The task of reaching the world is daunting at best. The missionaries cannot do it alone. God will, however, miraculously intercede, and hearts will be changed as missionaries work and as they are helped by our prayers. Remember the story of the battle the Israelites fought against the Amalekites as told in Exodus 17:8–13? Joshua and the army of Israel were winning when Moses held up his hands with the staff of God, but when he let down his hands, the enemy won. So Aaron and Hur held Moses' hands up—a clear witness of prayer as indicated in verse 16—and Israel won the battle. Prayer is the only way the Great Commission will be fulfilled. It can be done through prayer.

Your mission trip is over. You may go back some day and you may not. But your mission can continue! You can continue to assist the same missionaries. You can lift up the missionary's tired arms by your prayers and by encouraging others to join you. However, you will need to do some specific things to remind yourself to pray or busyness will make you forget. One man I know carries in his pocket a small coin from the country he visited. It is worth about 2/10 of one cent. Whenever he reaches for change to buy something and sees the coin, he is reminded to pray for the country, people, and missionaries who work there! As a truck driver, he spends a lot of time interceding for the country in which he served. A lady who visited a restricted-access country that grows a lot of olives cleaned olive pits and gave them to her teammates to carry as a prayer reminder. One country's leaders limit the sharing of the gospel. A major source of outreach there is via satellite TV. Satellite dishes are everywhere in the country and look a lot like mushrooms. So the visitors are encouraged to pray for the spread of the gospel every time they see mushrooms—on pizza, in salads, etc!

What are the everyday things and experiences you can use to remind you to pray for the missionaries in "your" country? Their hands may be heavy with fatigue or discouragement. You are not present with them, like Moses was not with Joshua. But you can help them win the battle today by your prayers. You see, they are *not* kidding. It is God's will to reach the world, and the missionary's dream is possible through his Spirit's working. Your prayer is God's plan for making this possible. Today!

WHEN YOU SEE THIS PENCIL USE YOUR JOURNAL TO MAKE MORE NOTES

MILE POST | 2

SHELTER FROM THE STORMS OF REENTRY
Howard and Bonnie Lisech, Deeper Roots

> "God is our refuge and strength, an ever-present help in trouble." Psalm 46:1

God is our shelter from the troubles of life. He is our strength; safety, courage, and rest are found in trusting him. Believers have no need to fear; almighty God is always present with them.

1. Read Psalm 46:1–3. How would you define the word "refuge"?

_____

2. How bad is the trouble the writer has described?

_____

3. What phrase indicates that facing trouble with confidence is a choice?

_____

4. Note in your own words the basis for the writer's confidence.

_____

5. How do you usually react to troubles and challenges that come into your life? What choices do you make? On what do you base those choices?

6. Read Habakkuk 3:17–19. Summarize the troubles described in these verses.

7. What attitudes and actions express Habakkuk's faith? Upon what does he base them? (For more of the basis of his faith, read Habakkuk 3:2.)

8. How can you apply this to your life to increase your faith?

9. In troubled times, there is a temptation to trust in our own resources rather than in God. Read 2 Chronicles 32:7–8. What did Hezekiah say that was so encouraging to the people?

10. Is this principle an encouragement to you? Explain.

11. Read Psalm 147:10–11. What do these verses say that pleases the Lord?

12. Are you trusting in God as your refuge and strength, or are you trusting in your own resources? In what areas of your life are you most tempted to place your trust instead of in him: education, intelligence, physical strength, beauty, or finances?

13. Perhaps you just don't know God well enough to place your confidence in him, and you may be afraid to trust him. According to Jeremiah 9:23–24, what should be the most important goal for your life? Is this your goal? Explain.

14. Can you say with confidence that God is your refuge and strength? Do you believe he is always present to help you in times

of trouble? What truth about God most encourages you to have confidence in him as your refuge and strength?

15. The Lord is ready to help. For the following verses, note the things that particularly encourage you to trust in the Lord and memorize your favorite.

Psalm 91:4–7

Psalm 115:11

Psalm 118:6

Psalm 146:5–6

Isaiah 41:13

Reflecting on your cross-cultural experience:

What was the most important thing you learned about God during your time overseas?

What do you remember most about the people you served there?

What would you rather forget?

Prayer Suggestions:

Thank the Lord for his faithfulness to you on your trip and ask him to help you if you feel overwhelmed, discouraged, or disconnected now that you are back home. Share your concerns and thoughts with the Lord. Ask him to help you understand and embrace the process you are going through.

(If you enjoyed this reentry devotional Bible study, check out www.DeeperRoots.com for information on the 14 day *Coming Home–Reentry Devotions For A Successful Return*, or *Coming Home Again–Reentry Devotions For Another Successful Return*.)

MILE POST | 3

1 Kings 18:17–46; 19:4

Elijah was one of Israel's greatest prophets. He lived at a time when the king of Israel was a wicked man who abused his power. Elijah, however, was a brave prophet who opposed the king even when it might cost him his life. One such encounter was on Mt. Carmel when Elijah challenged the false prophets to the duel of "fire from heaven." In the process, he challenged the spiritual decay in the household of the king.

It is a great story, especially the part where Elijah begins to tease the false prophets. "Where is your god?" he asks. "Is he on vacation? Has he gone to sleep?" (18:27). Be sure to read the passage, because no one can read it and not smile at the humor it contains.

By the end of the story, Elijah had been used by God to accomplish an amazing victory. God sent fire that consumed not only the sacrifice, but the wood, the water, the stones, and the dirt! I've seen rocks around a fire pit that have lasted for years, but these stones were reduced to ashes instantaneously. What a great victory! And what a great lesson for all those who were there.

However, we notice in the next chapter that Elijah ran into the desert and said, "Lord, take my life." He wanted to die. Wow! Elijah went from the glory of victory on the mountain to the depths of depression in the desert. And all this happened in one day!

We are made of flesh and blood, and sometimes our emotions are up and down. If you find yourself feeling down, what can you do? There are three things that will help you cope with depression.

First, remember that God is on his throne and remains in charge. There is a lot of comfort in knowing that God is not moved by moods. He is your rock and you can count on him. Remind yourself of his stability when your own moods betray you and you feel unstable.

Second, remember that you belong to him and nothing can change that. One privilege of being a child of God is knowing that whatever happens, you are always his. That is your very identity, and it cannot be changed by any circumstances here on earth.

Third, go help somebody else. I have a friend I visit frequently because he is a paraplegic and can't come to visit me. Sometimes when I go see Jack I'm down. But I never stay that way when I visit him. He always encourages me with his upbeat attitude, and I leave feeling glad I've spent time with him. One day Jack told me that after a visit, his "spirit soared." By reaching out to serve, I was blessed. By receiving my service, Jack was blessed. By our obedience, God was blessed. Go and do likewise.

MILE POST | 4

TRANSITIONING
Emily, short-term missionary with OMF International

As my year of serving in Taiwan drew to a close, I remember becoming overwhelmed with a heart of mixed emotions. For months I had looked forward to going home to see family and friends, breathing clean air, driving a car, eating American food, and communicating in English. As I returned home, however, I could not help but feel a deep sadness for all that I was leaving behind: close relationships, the Taiwanese church, beautiful mountains, and endless lessons God taught me through living in another culture. The experiences of being in Taiwan opened my eyes even wider to see the world in which he has placed me. Knowing that the Lord is my guide and is always present at my side helped ease the transition from being immersed in an Eastern culture to living once again in a Western culture. He alone knows all of the circumstances of life and is with me in each experience.

The apostle Paul, being a traveling missionary himself, knew what it was like to adapt to differing ways of life. To be in need, or to have plenty; to be well fed, or to be hungry; Paul knew that it was Christ who sustained him through all circumstances. May all of the transitioning times in our lives also push us to depend on the Lord who has all things in his hands.

Read Philippians 4:11–13

1. (a) In what ways are your physical circumstances changing as you return home?

   (b) In what ways are your cultural circumstances changing as you return home?

2. In verse 12, what is the secret of being content in all situations?

3. How can you rely on God to give you strength?

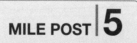

MILE POST | 5

EYES FOR OTHERS
Asher Sarjent, DELTA Ministries International

Philippians 2:3–11

> "Do nothing from selfishness or empty conceit, but with humility of mind let each of you regard one another as more important than himself."
> Philippians 2:3

I trust you found one of the strengths of your team's ministry was putting other's interests above your own—not only your teammates but those you went to serve as well. As we are directed in Scripture, we are not to think more of ourselves but are to look to the needs of others.

You can develop the same attitude that Christ possessed.

Check out a list of ways from God's Word that you can be an encourager:

Reference Example	Suggested Application
1 Thessalonians 5:11 Build each other up.	Point out to someone a quality you appreciate in him or her.
1 Thessalonians 5:12 Respect leaders.	Look for ways to cooperate.
1 Thessalonians 5:13 Hold leaders in highest regard.	Hold back critical comments about those in positions of responsibility. Say "thank you" to your leaders for their efforts.
1 Thessalonians 5:13 Live in peace.	Search for ways to get along with others.
1 Thessalonians 5:14 Warn the idle.	Challenge someone to join you in a project.
1 Thessalonians 5:14 Encourage the timid.	Encourage those who are timid by reminding them of God's promises.
1 Thessalonians 5:14 Help the weak.	Support those who are weak by loving them and praying for them.
1 Thessalonians 5:14 Be patient.	Think of a situation that tries your patience and plan ahead of time how you can stay calm.
1 Thessalonians 5:15/ Resist revenge.	Instead of planning to get even with those who mistreat you, do good to them.

1 Thessalonians 5:16 Be joyful.	Remember that even in the middle of turmoil, God is in control.
1 Thessalonians 5:17 Pray continually.	God is always with you—talk to him.
1 Thessalonians 5:18 Give thanks.	Make a list of all the gifts God has given you, giving thanks for each one.

MILE POST | 6

THE CART
Terri Hughes Vincelette, CultureLink
Dottie Connor Bingham, Gracestoration

"Come to Me ... all whose work is hard, whose load is heavy and I will give you relief. Bend your necks to my yoke, and learn from me, for I am gentle and humble-hearted: and your souls will find relief."
Matthew 11:28–29 NEB

Used by permission from Gracestoration

What do you see in the first frame of this picture? A mission trip can produce a lot of burdens to bear. What about the second picture? An opportunity for relief. Wouldn't you like some relief today from your burdens? Some rest? Look at the third frame. Do you see anything odd? What do you suppose the driver is thinking right now? The fourth frame shows the person still carrying burdens even though he got into the cart.

Teammates with different personalities; leaders who don't understand; crowded housing without personal space or time; exhaustion from ministry schedules; deep burdens for the lost; agony over the poverty; feelings of helplessness, anger, brokenness; missing someone back home; wondering about the future. These are some burdens that may be going through your heart and mind. These things can weigh heavy. Is there no rest?

The cart and horse represent Christ, our burden-bearer. "Praise be to the Lord, to God our Savior, who daily bears our burdens" (Psalm 68:19). Getting into the cart represents trusting Christ as Savior and burden-bearer. The good news is that the Lord desires to *continue* carrying all of your burdens. The person in the cart is expending needless energy. Do you ever feel like your energy is gone? Are you like that person in the cart, still carrying your own burdens? Christ wants to bear your burdens and give you rest. His rest is there for those who avail themselves of it. Isaiah 53:4 says, "Surely he took up our infirmities and carried our sorrows." Christ died not only to bear your sins upon the cross, but also to bear your sorrows, burdens, and griefs. Allow him to be your burden-bearer, and he will give rest for your soul.

> Let us cast all our burdens, and they are many and weighty, upon our omnipotent, all-wise, loving Father. They are but feathers to him!
>
> —Mrs. Hudson Taylor

> "Cast your burden upon the Lord, and he will sustain you; he will never allow the righteous to be shaken." Psalm 55:22 NASB

MILE POST | 7

MY GRACE IS SUFFICIENT FOR YOU
James from OMF International

2 Corinthians 12:9–10

What went wrong on your mission trip? Did travel delays leave you stranded? Were your teammates annoying? Was it hard to accept the ministry role you'd been given? Were you embarrassed or disappointed with your rough reaction to the new challenges? Did God show up when you needed him?

Disappointments and unmet expectations are a normal part of serving. Take a minute and look at Paul's response to his discouragements in 2 Corinthians 12:7–10. This is the passage where Paul talks about having a thorn in his flesh, a weakness that he feels very strongly. We're not told what this weakness is, only that Paul felt so burdened about it that he asked God to take it away three times.

Look at what God says to Paul in verse nine, "He has said to me, 'My grace is sufficient for you, for power is perfected in weakness.'" NASB

In what ways did you see God's grace providing for you when you needed it during your mission trip? Did he make some difficult challenges easier or help you overcome specific fears? Did he work through you despite your language limitations?

Look at Paul's response in verse ten, "Most gladly, therefore, I will rather boast about my weaknesses, that the power of Christ may dwell in me. Therefore, I am well content with weaknesses, with insults, with distresses, with persecutions, with difficulties, for Christ's sake; for when I am weak, then I am strong." NASB

Is this your message about your mission trip? What stories can you share to illustrate the power of Christ working in your weakness?

Maybe you're not sure that God's grace was sufficient. Sometimes the things you face in ministry situations seem like too much, especially if you're disappointed with yourself or with God. If this is how you feel, please talk with a ministry mentor about what you're feeling. You may be surprised how much perspective he or she can add to what you're feeling because of having had a similar experience.

MILE POST | 8

BALANCE AND BOUNDARIES
Bill Knepper, PastorShare, DELTA Ministries International

Philippians 2:1–11

> "Do nothing from selfishness or empty conceit, but with humility of mind regard one another as more important than yourselves." Philippians 2:3 NASB

The story is told of a man who was given a tour of hell. The tables were piled high with delicious food; roast turkey, mashed potatoes, fruit salads, and every kind of pie. However, he was shocked to see that all those sitting at the tables were thin and starving. He noticed they all had to use four-foot-long forks taped to their hands! They could see the food. They could even load the fork, but because it was so long, they could never get it to their mouths. They suffered in agony.

Then he was taken to heaven. Surprised, he saw the same thing! Tables loaded with food and forks four feet long taped to each person's hand. However, everyone was plump and happy. The difference was in what they did with the forks. Those in heaven fed each other.

It is not a surprise that the Scriptures command to "regard one another as more important than yourselves." This is at the very core of the Christian life. Being part of a team working in another country, you have experienced the value of cooperation, humility, forgiveness, and honoring others.

You may have a hundred new ideas to share now that you are home, but you must be careful to "regard one another" as you allow your enthusiasm to rub off on others. Remember those who sent you and stayed behind have not had the same experiences you have had. You have to let them experience it through you. "Regarding others" means that you are considerate of their feelings and respectful of their ideas. Enthusiasm is a wonderful thing and you don't want to lose it. So keep the balance and an "attitude the same as that of Jesus Christ" in all your dealings with others (Philippians 2:5).

MILE POST | 9

GLORIFYING GOD
Susan Barrett, Peacemaker Ministries

"So whether you eat or drink or whatever you do, do it all for the glory of God." 1 Corinthians 10:31

"Finally, brothers, whatever is true, whatever is noble, whatever is right, whatever is pure, whatever is lovely, whatever is admirable—if anything is excellent or praiseworthy—think about such things. Whatever you have learned or received or heard from me, or seen in me—put it into practice. And the God of peace will be with you." Philippians 4:8–9

Our short-term medical team was serving in remote villages in Honduras. The villages in which we were serving each day were plain and poverty-stricken, with dirt floors in the simple huts and water that had to be boiled before it could be used in the clinic. The living conditions were beginning to affect the attitudes of the team. We were tempted to complain or be grumpy with each other.

Our wise team leader decided to focus one of the morning devotionals on bringing glory to God in all circumstances. After reading the verses selected for the devotional time, the team discussed our human tendency to focus on our own desires and comforts, and what it would mean to rejoice in the Lord and bring praise to him.

As a group, we each shared what we might do to bring glory to God as we served. One of our nurses shared that she tried to hum a praise chorus and thank God for the thankful smiles on the villager's faces. Another team member expressed a desire to "look unto the hills" each morning to give praise for the mountain rainstorms that fed the brook running beside the village. One of the doctors gave thanks for the medicines that had been donated, some of which saved a village child's life the day before.

As the devotional ended we recognized that despite the circumstances in which we were working, when we paused to give God the glory in all things we were uplifted. Giving glory to God brought peace, and the potential conflicts of the day paled compared to what God was doing.

Challenge: What does it look like to bring glory to God in our own lives? Do we focus on God's glory rather than our own desires? Do we think about bringing God glory through the way we act, dress, or treat others before we think of our own comfort?

Reflect: What do you do in your everyday life to bring glory to God? Does this change if you are having a "tough" day or things are not going according to your expectations?

MILE POST | 10

EXAMINING MY OWN BEHAVIOR AND ATTITUDE
Susan Barrett, Peacemaker Ministries

> "If we claim to be without sin, we deceive ourselves and the truth is not in us." 1 John 1:8

Carol and Mary, short-term team members, were comparing notes after the evening team meeting to discuss the day's events and challenges.

"You know, I think my attitude needs adjusting," said Carol. "I was really complaining about the lack of team cooperation and the oppressive heat as we were working on the concrete project today. I was irritated with other team members, especially Ken, and I blamed my attitude toward him on the uncomfortable working conditions. After listening to the Scripture and discussion in tonight's meeting, I'm beginning to feel it's my sinful attitude and not the weather or working conditions that are causing my irritability. What do you think?"

"Well," replied Mary, "I'm not the Holy Spirit, but the lesson was speaking to me as well. When I snapped at George I blamed it on my lack of sleep. I really need to apologize to him and confess my sinful actions."

Carol continued, "Looks like we both need to confess. It's not easy for me to apologize but I realize it's the right thing to do. Will you pray for me as I plan and practice my apology to Ken for the way I treated him today?"

"I'll be glad to, if you'll do the same for me," said Mary.

Challenge: Instead of blaming others for a conflict or resisting correction, we need to trust in God's mercy and take responsibility for our own contribution. This includes confessing our sins to those we have wronged, asking God to help us change any attitudes and habits that have led to an ungodly response to conflict, and seeking to repair any harm we have caused.

Reflect: What do I need to examine in my own life, behavior, and attitude? Do I need to repent of slander, gossip, or an unloving attitude? What is God saying to me?

MILE POST | 11

FORGIVING OTHERS
Susan Barrett, Peacemaker Ministries

"Therefore, as God's chosen people, holy and dearly loved, clothe yourselves with compassion, kindness, humility, gentleness and patience. Bear with each other and forgive whatever grievances you may have against one another. Forgive as the Lord forgave you. And over all these virtues put on love, which binds them all together in perfect unity." Colossians 3:12–14

"It (love) is not rude, it is not self-seeking, it is not

easily angered, it keeps no record of wrongs."
1 Corinthians 13:5

"Be kind and compassionate to one another, forgiving each other, just as in Christ God forgave you." Ephesians 4:32

During a time of debriefing with her accountability partner, Jane shared that she was still angry with Brad. It was only a month since the short-term mission to Mexico, but Jane was still upset about the way Brad had embarrassed her in front of the rest of the team. When he apologized, she had said she would forgive him, but deep in her spirit she was still mad at him.

Her thoughts whirled as she began to share, "He should have known better than to embarrass me. He's always clowning around and making others look foolish. Why did he have to apologize in front of the rest of the team? I had to say I forgave him or I would have looked bad to the rest of the team. He deserves my anger. I'm still mad and I can't forget what he did."

Courtney listened and then said, "Let's see if we can look into God's Word for an answer to your dilemma." The two women read the verses from the New Testament listed above. As they did, Courtney prayed silently that the Holy Spirit would speak to Jane.

"How do these relate to what is going on with you, Jane?" Courtney asked in a quiet voice.

After a time of reflection, Jane responded, "I guess I'm working harder at staying mad at Brad than I am at forgiving him. I know I was embarrassed, but I guess if Jesus could go through the embarrassment and pain He did for me, I should be able to let go of my hurt and forgive Brad. This is a hard thing for me to do, Courtney."

"What do you think your first step should be?" replied Courtney.

"Well," Jane started, "the first thing is to ask God to forgive my sinful attitude—and then I'd better go to Brad and confess that I really didn't forgive him the first time."

"I agree," said Courtney.

Challenge: If Jane shared her thoughts with you, what would you have advised her to do? If you were Jane, what would you do next? Our call to peace mandates that we be people who forgive.

We forgive not because someone deserves to be forgiven but because we are to forgive as God forgave us. God forgave us because He loved us, not because we deserved it or even earned it!

When we forgive we make a promise not to continue to dwell on the incident, talk about the incident to others, use it against the other person, or allow the incident to hinder our relationship with the other person.

God models this kind of forgiveness. By his grace alone can we forgive others as he has forgiven us.

Reflect: Have I forgiven others because God commanded me to? Have I "let go" of a hurt because God expects me to? Have I allowed an incident to come between me and someone else? What is God telling me?

MILE POST | 12

CONFESSION
Susan Barrett, Peacemaker Ministries

"First take the plank out of your own eye."
Matthew 7:5

"If we confess our sins, he is faithful and just and will forgive us our sins and purify us from all unrighteousness." 1 John 1:9

"He who conceals his sins does not prosper, but whoever confesses and renounces them finds mercy." Proverbs 28:13

The best way to ruin a confession is to use words that shift the blame to others or that appear to minimize or excuse your guilt. The most common way to do this is to say, "I'm sorry if I've done anything to upset you." The word *if* ruins this confession, because it implies that you do not know whether you did wrong. The message you are communicating is this: "Obviously you're upset about something. I don't know that I have done anything wrong, but just to get you off my back I'll give you a token apology. By the way, since I don't know whether I have done anything wrong, I certainly don't know what I should do differently in the future. Therefore, don't expect me to change. It's only a matter of time before I'll do the same thing again."

Clearly this is no confession at all. It is a superficial statement designed to get someone to stop bothering you or to transfer fault for breaking a relationship.

Notice how the following so-called confessions are diluted by the words in italics:

"*Perhaps* I was wrong."

"*Maybe* I could have tried harder."

"*Possibly* I should have waited to hear your side of the story."

"*I guess* I was wrong when I said those critical things about you."

"I shouldn't have lost my temper, *but I was tired*."

Each of these statements would have value if the italicized words were left out. These words neutralize the rest of the confession and destroy its ability to convey sincere repentance and soften the heart of someone who has been offended. Therefore, make it a point to strike such words from your vocabulary any time you need to make a confession. (adapted from *PeaceMeal*, an e-letter from Peacemaker Ministries, 2005, used by permission)

Challenge: Confession is not easy, but it is an essential part of the restoration process. When confessing it is important to address everyone involved; avoid the words "if", "but" or "maybe"; admit the behavior or attitude specifically; acknowledge the hurt your behavior or attitude has caused; be ready and willing to accept the consequences for your behavior or attitude; be ready to identify and change the behavior or attitude that caused the hurt; and ask the injured party for forgiveness.

Reflect: Is there someone I need to go to and confess my part in a conflict? Even if I was the injured one, is there something I did to contribute to the problem? Can I ask for forgiveness without expecting someone else to make a confession?

MILE POST | 13

RECONCILIATION/RESTORATION
Susan Barrett, Peacemaker Ministries

"Therefore, if you are offering your gift at the altar and there remember that your brother has something against you, leave your gift there in front of the altar. First go and be reconciled to your brother; then come and offer your gift."
Matthew 5:23–24

"Be completely humble and gentle; be patient, bearing with one another in love. Make every effort to keep the unity of the Spirit through the bond of peace." Ephesians 4:2–3

"Do nothing out of selfish ambition or vain conceit, but in humility consider others better than yourselves. Each of you should look not only to your own interests, but also to the interests of others."
Philippians 2:3–4

The concrete delivery man is about to arrive with the first load of "mud" when John says to the team, "When the concrete gets here, load up your wheelbarrow and bring it over to me. I'll show you the best way to pour it."

"Wait a minute, John," says Ed. "Who died and made you boss? I'm the one with experience on a short-term team— been on four construction trips in two years. I should be able to tell everyone how to pour that mud."

"You've never been in *this* country before. Besides, I've poured concrete back home and have better judgment and experience than you do," retorts John.

"Look," Ed says, raising his voice, "you don't know what you're talking about. I have more and better experience."

"Let's take a break for a second, guys," interrupts Joel, the team leader. "I need to talk to John and Ed." On the side, Joel quickly says, "Can the two of you please cooperate? Let's share the responsibility and then we'll talk about your opinions once this pour is complete."

Both John and Ed grumble but get back to work with the rest of the team. Even though they don't look at each other for the time it takes to finish the pour, neither man continues their "I'm better than you" argument.

Later Joel asks both men to meet with him. Joel has them read Philippians 2:3–4 and then asks, "How do you think these verses apply to what went on today?"

Through gentle counseling Joel helped both men realize their selfish attitudes were the center of the conflict. He helped them to see their difference of opinion as an opportunity to seek a mutually satisfying solution without embarrassing the name of God by resorting to sinful responses. John and Ed confessed and reconciled with each other and apologized for their behavior to the rest of the team. (adapted from *The Team Peacemaker*, a short-term team preparation tool from Peacemaker Ministries, 2005, used by permission)

Challenge: Instead of accepting premature compromise and/ or allowing a relationship to wither, believers in Christ need to actively pursue peace and reconciliation. We need to be ready to forgive others as God is ready, through the sacrifice of Christ, to forgive us. Seeking just and mutually-beneficial solutions to our differences is the way we demonstrate our unity in Christ to those around us.

It is helpful to remember we are called not to merely listen to God's Word, but to obey it. When we respond to conflict in a sinful way we need to confess and seek reconciliation with those we have offended. As peacemakers, our prayer needs to be that our actions, attitudes, and service bring praise to our Lord and lead others to know his infinite love.

Reflect: Is there someone in my circle of family and friends I need to approach to restore a relationship that has withered or been damaged? What do I need to do next?

MILE POST | 14

SHORT-TERM MISSION — SHORT-TERM GLORY?
Adam Charon, STEMShare

> "He who speaks on his own does so to gain honor for himself, but he who works for the honor of the one who sent him is a man of truth; there is nothing false about him." John 7:18

You did it right. You left on your short-term mission promising to give God all the glory. When you came home, you made a point of giving God the glory in your reports. Now some time has passed. It's time for a check-up.

Since it was a short-term mission, does God get short-term glory? As short-term missionaries we can unconsciously round a corner where we feel that enough time has passed for God to get his glory, so now we can use "my trip" to get a little of our own. Ask yourself a few telling questions:

1. How am I talking about my short-term mission now that it is history?

2. Am I continuing to give God glory in the ways I speak

about it, or am I (consciously or unconsciously) finding ways to keep some of that glory for myself?

3. What's the motive behind what I'm sharing? Am I using my experience to improve my image? To influence others to think of me as brave and exciting?

There are other times when God's glory is best served by not saying much at all about your short-term mission, as may be the case with those who have been to a restricted-access nation. If you've been to a place where believers and missionaries could face persecution, you need to face this issue bluntly. If you are tempted to share sensitive information to let people know how brave you were, you could ultimately jeopardize the work, workers, or believers in that place.

Potential "Glory-Catchers"

I have served overseas.

How "great" or "awful" things are over there.

I had to endure amazing things.

I am now an "expert" about the people group to whom I ministered.

I can't tell you where I went, but I do want you to know that I am "God's Secret Agent."

Potential "Glory-Givers!"

In your personal life, continue to thank God for the deposit he has entrusted to you.

Put your experience to work for God's long-term glory! Align yourself with his end goal of worshippers from every tribe, tongue, and nation.

Champion the people group.

Champion the missionaries you worked with.

Further mobilize your church to pray, give, and go.

Father, deliver me from these little "glory-catchers." I seek and work for *your* honor and *your* glory, now and always! Amen.

ROCK-PILING
James from OMF International

Joshua 3–4

What was the "big moment" of your mission trip? Did you stand on top of a mountain (figurative or literal) you thought you couldn't climb? Was there a piece of the Bible that God opened to you in a new way? What did you learn about yourself that you had never thought about before? Did God give you the privilege of praying with a brand-new Christian? What happened that you will never forget?

When God was leading his people Israel out of Egypt, they had many of these moments. Can you think of a few? (Ten plagues, Red Sea, Mount Sinai, manna … Read Exodus for the full story.) Unfortunately, God's people quickly forgot these unforgettable events. Their mountain-top experiences with God didn't help their perspective with the next challenge. It's just like the Christian camp you may have gone to when you were growing up. The camp got you very excited about living whole-heartedly for God, but that lasted about fifteen minutes before you picked a fight with your brother on the drive home. In Israel's case, they complained and doubted so much that God eventually condemned them to 40 years of walking in the wilderness. This gave the whiners time to die off, and God hoped for better with the next generation. Fortunately for you, God doesn't always hand out 40-year punishments for forgetting what he's done.

Fast-forward to the book of Joshua. God is taking the new generation to their final destination, the Promised Land he committed to give them. As before, God opens this journey with a powerful demonstration of who he is. Read Joshua 3:1–5 and see the anticipation God is building. Finish reading Joshua 3 and see the powerful work God does on Israel's behalf.

Now this is where it gets interesting. God wants to give Israel a better chance of remembering his work this time around. Read Joshua 4:1–5. What a strange command! Why does God want rocks from the middle of the river? Weren't there plenty on the shore? Joshua 1:6–7 tells us the rocks are a memorial, a way to remember what God did. Imagine taking a walk with your dad and asking him about a strange pile of rocks by the river. What would it teach you to hear his powerful story that God stopped a river right on that spot to prove his faithfulness to your family? This is a little like the ticket stub you may have saved for your scrapbook, but on a much bigger scale! Not only is this large, it's designed to pass from generation to generation.

How will you build a memorial of this significant time in your walk with God? How will you continue to honor and praise God for what he did during your mission trip? Are you a writer? Keep journaling about your mission trip once you've returned. Can you write yourself a letter and have a friend send it to you six months from now? Are you a talker? Share with some close friends, or videotape yourself. Are there visible reminders you can place in your room or car?

What kind of rock-pile can you build to remind you of God's faithfulness and his work?

MILE POST | 16

WE MUST FINISH WHAT HE STARTED
Hans Finzel, WorldVenture

> "Then his disciples said to each other, 'Could someone have brought him food?' 'My food,' said Jesus, 'is to do the will of him who sent me and to *finish his work.* Do you not say, "Four months more and then the harvest?" I tell you, *open your eyes and look at the fields! They are ripe for harvest.*'" John 4:33–35 emphasis added

The twelve disciples were often clueless about what was going on right under their noses, as is illustrated in this story after the encounter with the woman at the well. Jesus never gave up on those chosen twelve. And despite *their* detours, Jesus always stayed on task. His passion on earth was to finish what he started. And I for one am glad that he did! We live in a world where people regularly break their commitments. Whether it is to a marriage, family, career, or friendship, people give up and flake out. But not the Jesus we follow. He went to the bitter end, straight to the cross for us. He certainly had times where he wanted to bail out, but he stayed the course through the finish line.

In this story of Jesus' meeting the woman at the well, he tells his disciples that his food, literally "meat, fulfillment, satisfaction," was to do the will of the Father. While the disciples were thinking about their stomachs, he was focused on the spiritual thirst of the woman.

We follow a finisher. He finished what he came to earth to do. Now it's our turn. The Lord passed on to us the Great Commission. He is looking for men and woman who consider it their fulfillment to do his will. At Jacob's well in Samaria, Jesus was consumed with talking to this woman. He saw right into her heart and knew that she had been married five times and was living with another man. He offered her the living water of the gospel. As it turned out, thanks to no help from the disciples, she and all her friends and many of her town received the forgiveness of his grace.

People all over the world are lost in spiritual darkness just like this woman. They are waiting for us to bring them the light of the gospel and the forgiveness of the living water of Jesus. It is easy to get off task and lose our burden for the needs of the world. We get serious about the Great Commission and then Monday morning happens. We get distracted by bills, studies, jobs, and relationships. We go on a short-term mission and are ready to sell out and save the world. Then we get home and the fire dies out. The distractions of this world always keep us from focusing on eternity.

I feel like I am very much like those first disciples. As the disciples sought to eat, Jesus wanted to deal with the spiritual needs of the Samaritan woman and her friends. "Stay on task," he challenged them. He rebuked them, "Open your eyes and look at the fields, they are white for harvest." He was speaking specifically about the woman and her friends, but the rebuke comes down through the centuries to us: stay focused on the real spiritual needs of those who cross our paths each day. Don't let the fire go out. Stay on task!

Application Prayer: I want to be part of finishing the task of sharing the gospel all over the earth. Lord, help me keep my eyes on the needs of the world so that my heart will reflect a burden for the harvest. Make me sensitive to the people who invade my space... They might just be the next women at the well.

MILE POST | 17

STARS IN THE UNIVERSE
Brian Heerwagen, DELTA Ministries International

Philippians 2:14–15; 4:11–13

The night sky is amazing sitting at 12,500 feet in the Andes Mountains near the village of Yala de Monte Carmelo, Argentina. Against the black backdrop of the universe, the stars shine in sharp contrast. The moon is so bright and so close it feels like I can reach out and touch it. It's not like that in the city where I live. In fact, I forget about the stars there. They are not seen most nights because of the glow of street lights, headlights, lit billboards, and storefronts. They are washed out. The extremes of the night sky are drowned out by light pollution.

The Apostle Paul, a man who once had everything, now sits in a small jail cell and writes, "Do everything without complaining or arguing so that you may become blameless and pure, children of God without fault in a crooked and depraved generation, in which you shine like stars in the universe" (Philippians 2:14–15).

Complaining, whether it is blatant, sarcastic, or shown through body language, is like light pollution and blurs the dividing lines between dark and light. When we complain, we look so much like the rest of the world that we lose our brilliance. We no longer appear in contrast to a hopeless generation, but we blend in. Our witness is compromised; life becomes increasingly unhappy.

On the other hand, our speech and conduct can be so crisp and above reproach that we are like the stars in the Argentinean night sky. We stand out clearly against the backdrop of a crooked and depraved generation.

The secret to a life free of complaining is a life filled with contentment. The secret to contentment is realizing our sovereign, loving God is fully aware of all our circumstances, and knowing we can do *all* things through Christ who gives us strength. He's the one we are to talk to about our troubles. He understands, and he is the one with the power to change the circumstances … or to change us.

Is your life like the stars in the night sky of the mountains or the dull blur of the city? Does your life communicate hope, contentment, and faith in the power of Christ? Trust the Lord for contentment. Talk to him about your troubles instead of complaining to others. People will notice a difference.

MILE POST | 18

EXPECTATIONS BASED ON TRUTH
Howard and Bonnie Lisech, Deeper Roots

Trust in the LORD with all your heart and lean not on your own understanding." Proverbs 3:5

There is nothing wrong with having expectations. But an expectation must be based on the truth of God's Word. Often our personal expectations are not based on truth, but rather on something imagined or wished for. These unrealistic expectations can cause us to be disappointed, discouraged, and even angry. Our godly attitude can instantly change to one of ungodliness if our expectations are not met. Expectations usually have their root in our desire to control our circumstances or other people. This desire is not from God but is a work of the sin nature of man.

1. Read 2 Kings 5:1–15. According to verses 10–11, what were Naaman's expectations when he arrived at Elisha's house?

(a) Why do you think Naaman expected a big display?

(b) Why do you think Elisha did not permit a spectacle?

(c) How does Naaman handle his unrealistic, unmet expectation?

(d) What logic does he use to justify his sin in his own mind?

(e) According to verse 14, what action of Naaman illustrates an acceptance of his circumstances?

(f) If Naaman had insisted on controlling his circumstances, what would he have missed?

(g) How did Naaman's obedience and humility give glory to God?

(h) If Elisha had met Naaman's expectations for a spectacle and if he thought it was Elisha who had healed him instead of God, what do you think would have been the end result?

(i) What influence do you think Naaman had on those who witnessed this event?

2. Are you ever like Naaman? If so, in what way?

3. Have you ever manipulated your circumstances to have your expectation met? Explain.

4. In verse 13, Naaman listens to the *wise* counsel of his servants. Why is this a good principle to remember when you are angry and disappointed because of an unmet expectation?

5. What do you think were Naaman's attitudes when he finally chose to wash in the Jordan?

6. In 2 Kings 5:12, Naaman's anger and disappointment lead him to rely on his own reason and logic to determine how he was going to handle his unmet expectation. Read Proverbs 3:5–7. Write each phrase and its *meaning*.

vs. 5a

vs. 5b

vs. 6a

vs. 6b

vs. 7a

vs. 7b

7. When unexpected things occur in our lives, what happens when we choose to obey the spiritual principles found in question #6?

8. God's actions are delayed at times. Sometimes we don't receive what we expect because God has something better planned for us. Read John 11:1–6, 11–15, 17–45.

(a) What did Mary and Martha expect?

(b) Why did Jesus delay?

(c) How did God's actions exceed their expectation?

(d) What was the result?

9. Naaman, Mary, and Martha each chose to surrender and obey, denying and dying to their own way and will. They began to trust and know God. In the same way, believers must deny themselves, surrender, and die to their self-life. These moment-by-moment decisions will result in a deeper trust and more intimate relationship with God. Write your thoughts.

Reflecting on your cross-cultural experience:

Did you return from your overseas experience with a grateful heart? List the things for which you are grateful.

While overseas, was there a difficult experience that you now consider with thanksgiving?

Prayer Suggestions:

Praise the Lord that he is your all-knowing and all-mighty God. Express your desire to relinquish control of your life circumstances and your unrealistic expectations to him. Personalize and pray back to God the words of Proverbs 3:5–7. Thank him for the truth of his Word and for his willingness to bless you and glorify himself far beyond your expectations. Share your concerns and thoughts with the Lord. Ask him to help you understand and embrace the process you are going through.

(If you enjoyed this reentry devotional Bible study, check out www.DeeperRoots. com for information on the 14 day *Coming Home–reentry Devotions For A Successful Return*, or *COMING HOME AGAIN–Reentry Devotions For Another Successful Return*.

SALTY SALT

by a Christian worker on the field, International Mission Board (Southern Baptist Convention)

In a culture where there is no electricity and people have to hunt and gather food on a daily basis, people use air-drying and salt to preserve their food. It's done much the same as it was during the days when our Lord walked the earth and spoke to the disciples from the top of a mountain. Jesus told the disciples (and us) how to live in order to be blessed. After those famous beatitudes, he told us that if we walk according to those precepts, we are salt. Salt isn't just used to flavor food (though it does make it tastier and serves to enhance food's natural flavors). In Jesus' day, it was used to preserve food that would perish. So, if salt lost its saltiness it *was* good for nothing. If the salt loses its savor you've just lost a whole goat! Around here, a goat costs more than a month's wages.

So whenever I go on village visits, I am interested to see the clotheslines hung with strips of thinly sliced meat. The meat is usually rubbed with a bit of oil and then salted before being hung to dry. After dried, it's pounded into a powdery beef jerky stuff and used in a sauce called sharmoot (which is delicious, by the way). What if the meat isn't properly taken care of? It is usually rotten, and the sauce tastes and smells horrible and can make you very sick.

The salt helps to preserve that which is *destined* to rot and make it into something good and useful. So it is with us—those of us who believe and follow the one true King. Looking around at corruption, at squalor, at incredibly impoverished living conditions, we see that this place *needs* salt. And it needs salty salt. That starts right here with us, I dare say. So please pray for us to be salty in this needy land. Pray for God to send more salty laborers to work alongside us to preserve more people from corruption and decaying lifestyles on earth and eternity in the rotten stench of hell.

How will you be salt today? The nations are all around you.

How will you bring flavor to the lives of those around you so they know the richness of our Lord? Write down some practical ways you will be salty salt in your world this week.

Write a prayer asking the Lord where he wants you to spread your saltiness—on mission in your hometown? Around your state? Around the world?

Find a mission project and pray for God to send salty messengers so that his name and salvation will be made known among the nations. Ask the Lord if you are to be part of that project.

"You are the salt of the earth." What's your plan to flavor those around you today?

MILE POST | 20

REVIEWING WHAT GOD IS DOING
Matt Paschall, DELTA Ministries International

Philippians 1:6

I would have never taken *him* on a short-term mission project—he was spiritually immature, his parents were going through a painful divorce, he was stubborn, self-absorbed, undisciplined, and untested. But fortunately, my youth pastor saw God working in my life. I went to Mexico for the first time as a student team leader at age 16, and this event radically changed my life. It was there in the rural village of Algadonez (near Yuma, Arizona) that I was given the privilege of leading two young boys to the Lord. For the first time, I believed God could use me and call me to his service, even if I didn't have my act together. Almost 20 years have gone by since that experience as a teenager There have been many other events since then that have helped to shape who I am today.

It is good to reflect on how and when God has caused growth in your life. In the Old Testament they used to build memorials signifying key spiritual turning points in people's lives. I am not one to journal regularly, but I usually keep a written record of the memories, life-lessons, and answered prayers from my various missions projects. When I look back at the pictures and read through the journals, I am reminded of how far I have come while also seeing how far I have to go. Though we never fully arrive this side of heaven, there should be areas of Christ-likeness developing in our lives.

The danger of some who participate in short-term mission projects is that they try to gauge their walk with Christ based on their performance during the project. But our confidence needs to be based upon God's faithfulness rather than in our ability to serve him. "In all my prayers for all of you, I always pray with joy because of your partnership in the gospel from the first day until now, being confident of this, that he who began a good work in you will carry it on to completion until the day of Christ Jesus" (Philippians 1:4–6).

When Paul prayed for the church in Philippi, he rejoiced over their salvation and growth. He knew that what Christ had begun in their lives would be completed, for Christ is the author and finisher of our faith. He went on to pray that they might live full lives; that they might be faithful in their daily walk; and that they might be fruitful in Christian service. This was a prayer for Christian maturity.

In another verse, Paul challenges the church to have a kingdom perspective on character. "May God himself, the God of peace, sanctify you through and through. May your whole spirit, soul and body be kept blameless at the coming of our Lord Jesus Christ. The one who calls you is faithful and he will do it" (1 Thessalonians 5:23–24).

When we remain obedient and our hearts are open to being molded by his Spirit, then God is able to work through us supernaturally to accomplish his unique assignments for our lives.

Extra Step: Review your last short-term mission project or area of service. Where does God seem to be working in your life to make you more like Jesus?

BUT I DON'T HAVE TIME TO LOVE MY NEIGHBOR...

David Jensen, Initiatives International

Serving others is central to the Christian faith. Jesus said that to love the Lord our God with all our heart, soul, mind, and strength is the first and greatest commandment. Second only to that, he said we are to love our neighbors as we love ourselves. All the Law and the Prophets hang on these two commandments (Matthew 22:37–40).

Now those are cross-cultural words for us to hear. Our culture reinforces the idea that "looking out for number one" is our highest priority. So how do we live in such a way that we make serving others our priority? There are so many demands on our time. How do we simplify our lives to the point that, like the Good Samaritan, we can and will go out of our way to serve others? I don't know about you, but I find that I'm much more willing to be interrupted and to help someone else when I'm not overworked, overstressed, and trying to operate at 125% of capacity. Did you know that Americans work more and take less vacation than most other nations? Where will we find the time and energy to serve others when we are exhausted from our work and home responsibilities?

Isn't Jesus to be our example on this quest toward balanced and holy living? Mark 10:45 reminds us, "For even the Son of Man did not come to be served, but to serve, and to give his life as a ransom for many." Now Jesus, more than any of us, was on a mission with eternal significance. And yet, he came to serve. He looked beyond himself and served the people around him. It makes me wonder how significant most of the things on my to-do list really are.

Short-term mission offers us an invitation to look beyond our own world. It calls us to experience someone else's reality and to give generously of ourselves. Do we have to go to distant lands to serve others? Of course not! But it is often on the journey to places that are far away and uncomfortable to us that we begin to see God, ourselves, and the world more clearly. (God often took his servants on journeys when he wanted to get their attention.) We begin to connect the dots between living a life of service while on a STM, and living that kind of life here at home.

My 16-year-old son is a great example of a person who has made those connections. He just naturally looks out for others. At 16, he has already gone on two short-term missions to work on Indian reservations in South Dakota. He has gone to Mexico multiple times to help build churches and to care for children in orphanages. His developing social conscience got him involved in a sleep-out to raise money and awareness for the homeless in our city. He typically spends each Halloween staffing a safe and fun carnival for hundreds of neighborhood kids, and spends time every week with fifth and sixth grade boys at our church. Even his friends recognize that Jon will "always do his best for someone else."

That's how I'd like to be known—as a person who gave himself to serve others. Is that the kind of reputation that you are developing at home, after having experienced so much joy in serving others while on your STM? Do you need to clear some things out of your schedule in order to find your meaningful place of service?

MILE POST | 22

THE LONG CHAIN OF OBEDIENCE
Hans Finzel, WorldVenture

> "Then Jesus said to Simon, 'Don't be afraid; from now on you will catch men.' So they pulled their boats up on shore, *left everything and followed him.*" Luke 5:10—11 emphasis added

Of all the decisions in the New Testament, one of the most far-reaching is found in Luke Chapter 5 when Jesus calls his first followers. The decision those fishermen made that day on the shore of Galilee directly affects our lives. It was the beginning of a *long chain of obedience*. Would I be a follower of Jesus today if they had not answered his call that day? Would the message have ever gotten to me?

The fishermen, who were experts at catching fish, had fished all night and come up empty-handed. Jesus, who on the other hand was a carpenter, had borrowed their boat to teach that morning. At the end of his teaching time, he asked the fishermen to take their boats back out and try again to catch some fish. They had already cleaned their equipment. It was time to go home for a late breakfast. They absolutely *knew* that they were going to catch nothing that day. After all, it was now already the middle of the day. Nobody catches fish at high noon! Reluctantly they obeyed him ... and it changed their lives forever.

Jesus loved to use real life to teach great truth. The men caught so many fish, their boats began to sink. Christ certainly performed this miracle to demonstrate that he is the Lord of the universe, Lord of the lake, and Lord of the fish. The vivid reality of a boat full of flopping fish perfectly illustrated Jesus' purpose in that afternoon of fishing: "Don't be afraid for *from now on you will catch men*." Not only was he demonstrating his great power and authority over all creation, but he was also calling them to a much higher calling than their careers as fishermen. Though they were successful as fishermen, they were about to move on to much greater significance. How many of us are trapped in jobs and lives that give us some degree of *success* ... but we crave more *significance*? *Success* is of this world, *significance* is of the next. When Jesus calls us into his service, he calls us into that great transition from *success to significance.*

I've often wondered what would have happened to the church if these men had not responded positively to Christ's call that day. Luke tells the story: "They pulled their boats up on shore, left everything, and followed him." They left their boats, they left their nets, and they even left the fish. Christ must have really broken through to their hearts that day for them to leave everything behind. They literally walked away from their professions that day—left their livelihoods lying on that shore.

Working in the harvest on the mission fields of the world is a ministry of tremendous eternal significance. But it doesn't happen without leaving something behind. We have to obey his call to move from success to significance. And that movement requires us to go out of our comfort zones. I'm so very thankful for those fishermen who made that profound decision that day to leave everything and follow Jesus. They began a long chain of obedience that has stretched through the centuries as men and women have continued to obey that call to leave the world behind and to follow Jesus. Today he calls us to join that chain.

Application Prayer: Am I willing to leave everything I love and follow you? Lord, I want significance out of my life as I follow you. Please help me see how I am to become part of the long chain of obedience to spread your message around the world. Show me what I need to let go of so that I can embrace this call on my life. Help me grab that chain and not let go.

MILE POST | 23

WHEN THE GOOD NEWS IS A TOUGH CHOICE
George Siler, Student Minister at Faith Baptist Church, Memphis, Tennessee.

Jeremiah 21:1–9

"Tara was only in the seventh grade when she secretly enrolled in a Bible correspondence school. Her strict Muslim family later discovered her faith in Jesus and beat her so severely that she lay unconscious for almost a week. Tara eventually had to flee her home and her country of Pakistan to escape certain death." (Steve Cleary)*

Sometimes the Good News is not an easy choice. When King Zedekiah finally sent for the prophet Jeremiah to give him a word from God, it was because the Babylonian army was parked outside his gates. For too long he had ignored the threat of judgment. Now he was desperate for good news from the Lord's prophet.

Jeremiah responded, "Good news! I have some good news! This city is going to fall and you with it. You can expect nothing from the enemy but the sword, fire, pestilence, and famine." Then Jeremiah added this bit of hope: "Oh yes, did I say that if you surrender yourselves to the Babylonians, you get a chance to live? It's your choice: fight and die, or surrender and trust God."

That was not what the king and his advisors wanted to hear. To the last, they refused to humble themselves before God.

We might have little sympathy for Zedekiah, but there are many in today's world who face a difficult choice when they hear the Gospel. They must go against godless governments, false religions, and even family members if they embrace Christ as Lord. We are amazed by the faith of believers in China who choose imprisonment and torture rather than betray their house church to the state. Christians die daily in places like Sudan, Tajikistan, Indonesia, and Pakistan. The Good News is precious, however, even when it is dangerous.

Whether your mission trip leads you to an American city, a Mexican village, or a Middle Eastern refugee camp, don't ever be casual about the message of salvation. The choice for someone may be more difficult than you know.

Pray as Jesus did for the protection of Christians who face persecution for following him. In John 17: 11, 14–18, Jesus asks God not to take his children out of the world, but to protect them from the evil one by the power of his name. We can speak that same prayer on behalf of persecuted believers this very moment.

Jesus knew the cost of being true to his calling—torture and death. He also knows the cost of following him in many parts of our world. Ask God to give to persecuted Christians the same courage that Jesus had to face his tormentors and the torture of his death.

If you are interested in reading more about those who have encountered persecution for the cause of Jesus Christ, consider reading the following:

1) *Jesus Freaks,* DC Talk and The Voice of the Martyrs

2) *The New Foxe's Book of Martyrs,* John Foxe

3) *Hebrews 11,* The Holy Bible

*Cleary, Steve. "Extreme Youth" in The Voice of the Martyrs newsletter, 12/2001, p.10

MILE POST | 24

BEGGING TO GIVE
Brian Stark, DELTA Ministries International

2 Corinthians 8:1–15

My wife and I have been involved in support-based ministry since we left Bible college. In many ways, it is all we have ever known. Asking people to pray about being involved financially in our ministry is a common thing for us. Yet, despite asking other people to give from their finances to our ministry, we always excused our own lack of financial involvement in others' ministries. We tithed to our local church, but said that our "extra" giving was the financial sacrifices we were making to be vocational ministers.

Thankfully, that is not the example we have been shown by the churches in Macedonia in 2 Corinthians 8:2–4. "Out of the most severe trial, their overflowing joy and their extreme poverty welled up in rich generosity. For I testify that they gave as much as they were able, and even beyond their ability. Entirely on their own, they urgently pleaded with us for the privilege of sharing in this service to the saints."

Their extreme poverty overflowed in rich generosity! They begged Paul to be able to give! How easy to say we don't have enough or we cannot give. Yet God doesn't expect us to give according to what we do *not* have, but according to what we *do* have (see 2 Corinthians 8:12).

God does not expect my family to give in the same manner as the successful business owner or doctor in my church would be able to. However, he does expect my family to give, whether we think we can afford it or not.

One of the families that supported us in the early years was an excellent example to us. When money got tight and they were not sure they could pay all the bills, the father would say, "Money is tight this month, we better give more!"

This last year we started giving to three different ministries over and above our tithe. Many months I could easily see how we needed that money for something else, and questioned whether we would have enough. Yet as we have faithfully given to our church and these three ministries first, God has proven himself faithful in meeting every need … not necessarily the wants, but always the needs.

You've been to the field, you've seen the needs, you've seen how far your few dollars can go, and you've seen how rich you truly are compared to the rest of the world. Will you allow God to use your resources to further that ministry or maybe another ministry?

Get on your knees and ask God what you should give and to whom, and then follow through on that commitment. Will you beg God to allow you to give?

MILE POST | 25

I WILL REMEMBER THE DEEDS OF THE LORD
James from OMF International

Psalm 77

The Psalms are powerful places of expressing feelings to the God you follow. Amazingly, almost every kind of emotion is shared, from the highest joys to the most despondent lows. Sometimes the writer doesn't even bother to separate his conflicting emotions into unique Psalms. Psalm 77 seems to swing through extremes faster than an explosive reality-TV show. Read verses 1–9 and sum up what the author is expressing to God.

Are there times you've had pretty much the same message in your conversations with God?

Now skip down and read verses 13–20. How would you describe these same emotions in a letter to a friend?

So this leads to an obvious question. Why is there such a massive difference between the writer's perspective in verses 1–9 and verses 13–20? What happens in those middle verses, and where do you sign up to get some more? OK, read verses 10–12.

What does the writer do that changes his perspective so deeply?

He spends time looking back on what God has done in the past and remembering who God is. Is this just some kind of self-help session about the power of positive thinking? Is it an attempt to escape reality through thinking about the good old days? No. The change agent here is reflection on who God is, expressed through his faithfulness in the past. What you see in Psalm 77 is one man working through a perspective change as he remembers God's character. The reflections on the past are powerful because they tell about who God is today.

Do you have stories of God's work to remember; the kind of stories you built a Joshua 4 rock-pile around? No matter how excited you feel, there will be discouragements ahead. This is especially true if you continue to serve God. Are you ready to reflect on God's character in these times? Do you believe he is faithful enough to pull you through times like verses 1–9? Will you choose to praise him when you feel like he's abandoned you?

MILE POST | 26

TODAY!
Andy Spohrer, WorldVenture

Today! Yes, the future is important and I do need to plan and work for the future. How does God want me to invest my life? What place should global evangelism have in my planning? How should I prepare for that possibility? And on and on the questions go. But what about today? What does God want me to do today?

Recently I was struck while reading Psalm 101. Yes, we all know Psalm 100 and sing the first phrase often. Some of us love the KJV wording of "make a joyful noise" because that is all our singing is! But because we know and love Psalm 100, I think we often skip over the one that follows, and this is our loss. For here we see David saying that he will not only sing praise to God, but that he will seek to lead a "blameless" life at home! Wow, right in front of those who know him best. He is determined to live a life that is blameless right in the place where he lets down and relaxes! That can be the place where being a Christian is the hardest. Notice how he sees this impacting his life. Verse 2 speaks of his walk at home being blameless. Verse 3 talks about what he looks at! He will not let evil deeds cling to him. Have you seen deeds on TV that you have started to own or at least defend? Are you, like me, sometimes embarrassed to realize you are cheering for the likeable character to succeed in his adultery or whatever just because he seems so nice?! What values cling to you after seeing what you see?

In verse 5 David says he will not listen to someone slandering his neighbor. How easy it is to listen to gossip, and to take part in it. And how easy it is to fish for more information. It is often a favorite sport of Christians to criticize those who are different from us. How can I pray for the salvation of someone I am slandering? Is this the way I love my neighbor? Haughty eyes and a proud heart either allow us to slander or follow—either way they surely go together. And God hates those with haughty eyes (Proverbs 6:17)! It is far easier to focus on the failures of others than to deal with our own imperfections. Verse 6 shows that he values the faithful person. Do we show our appreciation for the one who is quietly serving God? Do I hang out with that kind of person?

Like you, I have a passion for reaching our world for Christ and for seeing more people sent into the harvest. Planning and preparing for that occupies much of my time and energy. But it is critically important that *today* I am also occupied with honoring God in my home! Perhaps this is the greatest missionary challenge there is. After all, it determines the kind of person I am and am becoming, which determines whether or not I have a message worth sharing around the world!

FINDING A PARTNER
David Jensen, Initiatives International

"Charm is deceptive, and beauty is fleeting; but a woman who fears the LORD is to be praised."
Proverbs 31:30

Will I ever find a partner? How will I know? While this verse and the passage in which it is found (Proverbs 31:10–31) are written from the perspective of a man looking for a wife of noble character, they speak to anyone thinking about finding a life partner. The message is the same for all of us. Internal character is always more important and long-lasting than external appearance. While physical attractiveness may play a part in bringing couples together, it has little to do with what keeps couples together.

Working with college students for 15 years, I've had many conversations about dating and marriage. It is an important topic that deserves consideration. It can frequently arise during and following a short-term mission experience, especially for young, single adults who have experienced a clarification of values during the STM.

Here are a few suggestions to keep in mind when thinking about who you will marry someday:

1. Go slow! It takes time to build any relationship, and it is dangerous to move too fast. You can't really *know* a person quickly. Protect yourself from attaching too soon and remember that your hormones can deceive you during the first 3–6 months of a romantic relationship.

2. Build friendships! Exclusive dating relationships are not necessarily the ideal goal. We all need friends of both genders, regardless of our age or marital status. If an exclusive relationship does emerge at some point, your solid friendship will serve you well.

3. Become a person of noble character yourself! Don't be afraid

to do some hard work on your personal growth and development. What are your strengths and weaknesses? What are your own dreams and passions? These are important questions to answer before worrying about finding a mate.

4. Be inclusive, not exclusive! Seek to include others in all of your relationships. Remember you are a member of the body of Christ, and there is no one person who can meet all of your relational needs. We need each other.

5. Use your head when dating! Drs. Les and Leslie Parrott call this "dating smart." In their book, *Relationships*, they explain what is involved in smart dating. I highly recommend it. You can find all their resources at www.realrelationships.com

2 Corinthians 6:14 tells us "not to be yoked together with unbelievers." This verse doesn't just refer to marrying a non-Christian. It speaks of the importance of finding a partner who shares your heart values. Are you a good match on things that matter most? Shared experiences, like a short-term mission, are actually good ways to find out about a person's values and core beliefs. Does the description in Proverbs 31:20 apply? "She opens her arms to the poor and extends her hands to the needy." There is little support for the "opposites attract" belief, except perhaps in the area of personalities. Sharing a meaningful spiritual journey with someone who cares about the same things that matter most to you is an important ingredient in building a marriage that lasts. A bad marriage is *never* better than no marriage at all!

MILE POST | 28

A CHILD WHO THREW A ROCK
Chris McDaniel, DELTA Ministries International

Luke 19:17
2 Corinthians 8:3–4

In the late 1800's Hattie May Wiatt, a young girl in Pennsylvania, attended a very small church that was regularly overcrowded. She had heard that future plans included building a larger church and Sunday school room. Soon after learning this, she got very sick and died. After the child's funeral, her mother brought 57 cents to the pastor. Hattie May had set aside this money in a bag as her contribution toward a larger facility that could hold more children. The pastor took the gift to the members of the church and stated that they had received their first contribution toward a larger facility. He then changed the money into 57 pennies and offered them for sale. All 57 pennies sold for about $250.00. The Pastor then took the $250.00 and changed all of it into pennies, offering them for sale as well. From the sale of these pennies, they received enough to buy the house next door.

This initial gift of 57 cents led to the formation of the Wiatt Mite Society, whose purpose was to enlarge upon the first 57 cents given by Hattie May. Over time, influenced by this young child's gift, they were able to raise substantial funds as the congregation grew. By 1912, the church grew to over 5,600 members.

It was in this same church that several institutions known today were founded; Samaritan Hospital (now called Temple University Hospital) which has helped cure and minister to thousands of people, as well as Temple University, which has educated over 80,000 young people.

The thought of such a "Ripple Effect" is almost beyond our comprehension. God used a little girl with a faithful and obedient heart to "throw a rock" and start a ripple that continues to this day. What an amazing privilege! Did you know that God uses you and me in this same way? He bestows upon his people the great honor of being participants in his work. We don't deserve such things.

God does much through humble people who are faithful in small ways. You have experienced this first-hand through support discovery for your mission trip. Every gift, no matter how large, was a rock that started a ripple in your life and the lives of those impacted through your ministry. Your support team was made up of God's people who were faithful and obedient in small ways and who understood the great privilege of participating in his work.

In Luke 19:17, the Lord stresses the importance of being faithful in small matters and how that faithfulness leads to more responsibility. Today, let each of us pray for the strength to be faithful and obedient in small ways, and praise God for the undeserved privilege of being used by him to accomplish his eternal plan.

Information taken from: **The History of 57 Cents**, Russel H. Conwell. The Temple Review, Grace Baptist Temple, Philadelphia, December 19, 1912.
Source: http://www.library.temple.edu/collections/special_collections/hattie.htm

MILE POST | 29

WE CAN DO SMALL THINGS WITH GREAT LOVE
Hans Finzel, WorldVenture

"When Jesus landed and saw a large crowd, *he had compassion on them*, because they were like sheep without a shepherd. So he began teaching them many things." Mark 6:34

"Praise be to the God and Father of our Lord Jesus Christ, the *Father of compassion* and the God of all comfort." 2 Corinthians 1:3

"Therefore, as God's chosen people, holy and dearly loved, *clothe yourselves with compassion*, kindness, humility, gentleness and patience." Colossians 3:12

Visiting Calcutta, India for the first time, I was stunned by the squalor of the slums. I prayed selfishly, "Lord, thank you that I was not born into this misery." As I traveled mile after mile through the filth and dirt of the homeless shantytowns, I thought,"How could anyone make a difference here? I could spend my life in this city and no one would notice. It would be like putting my finger in the ocean to move the water." Then I went to the compound of Mother Teresa and found my answer. She won the 1979 Nobel Peace Prize for her impact on this city and the world. This small, fragile woman said, "We cannot do great things on this earth. We can only do small things with great love."

Acts of compassion should be a part of all missionary work. In fact, Jesus Christ spent more time *touching* and healing people than he did *talking* to them. Check it out for yourself. Read through the four gospels and mark verses where he is *talking to the masses* with one color and where he is *touching people with acts of compassion* with another. So often we think that missions is throwing words at people. But sometimes their bellies are screaming so loudly with hunger that our voices are drowned out. We can follow the example of our own Lord Jesus Christ who constantly met human need as he shared the good news of the gospel. *Talking and touching* are the two principle activities of effective missionary strategy. Yes, we need to verbalize the truths of the gospel and, yes, we need to teach followers to be disciples. But at the same time, touching human needs by our acts of compassion will strengthen our message, and we can bless those who are much less fortunate than we.

How can we touch our audiences with acts of compassion? Housing abandoned street kids in Sao Paulo. Building new homes for the Tsunami victims of Southeast Asia. Providing fresh water supplies for tribes in Kenya. Sponsoring children at risk in Thailand. Teaching trades to those without a means of livelihood in Africa. Building and staffing clinics and hospitals for those without medical care. Providing basic education to slum-dwellers in Beirut so they can have a better future. These are some of the acts of compassion I have witnessed first-hand around the globe.

It was Saint Francis who said, "Preach the gospel at all times, and if necessary, use words." I have always loved those words as a reminder to help people where they hurt. Then they will listen to my words.

Application Prayer: Lord, I cannot change the world all by myself. But I can do small acts of kindness along the way. Teach me how to be an empathetic messenger of the gospel. Show me how to put the touch of grace into my mission strategy. Help me balance the sharing of words with the showing of compassion.

MILE POST | 30

MAINTAINING A POSITIVE TESTIMONY
Bill Knepper, PastorShare, DELTA Ministries International

Galatians 2:11–14

> "When Peter came to Antioch, I opposed him to his face, because he was clearly in the wrong."
> Galatians 2:11

It must have been a tense moment in the life of the early church. The apostle to the Jews (Peter) was confronted by the apostle to the Gentiles (Paul). It could have been explosive and resulted in the first major split in the church. If Peter had decided to defend himself, or if Paul had been personal and ugly in his charge, this might have been a deathblow to the early church. But that isn't what happened. Peter was wrong, and maybe more important to our story, it appears he submitted to Paul's rebuke (as corroborated by Peter's later assertion that Paul was to be obeyed. See 2 Peter 3:15-16).

It isn't easy to live the Christian life. It might be free, but it costs you everything you have. Sometimes we make mistakes, and sometimes those who see the mistakes confront us. Our attitudes should be like Peter, admitting when we are wrong and making it right.

We can do a lot to avoid the mistakes, however, by being careful how we live. Even in little things we should avoid the appearance of evil. When others look at our rooms, our computers, inside our lockers, on the back of our t-shirts, or on the bumpers of our cars, do they see things consistent with our love for Jesus Christ?

A man worked for several years for a bank, and the bank president noticed his good work. The day had come to announce to the man that he was going to be promoted to vice-president of the bank. The president took him out to lunch with plans to tell him the good news over a meal. However, standing behind the man in the cafeteria line, he noticed that he slipped a five-cent pat of butter under his bread so the cashier wouldn't see it. The president concluded that a man who would steal five cents' worth of butter might steal from the bank itself. He never made the offer of vice-president.

You do not know who is looking at you and studying how you live. Someone once said, "You are the only Bible that some people will ever read." Don't take shortcuts with the truth. Don't compromise on things you know are wrong. Don't let anyone have any doubt that you are a sold-out, satisfied servant of the living God.

MILE POST | 31

GUARD YOUR HEART
Howard and Bonnie Lisech, Deeper Roots

"Above all else, guard your heart, for it is the wellspring of life." Proverbs 4:23

In the King James Version, this verse says, "Keep thy heart with all diligence: for out of it are the issues of life." "Heart" can also be translated as *mind*, which includes a person's spirit, intellect, and will. The heart determines thoughts, actions, and values.

According to Proverbs 4:23, how much effort should believers exert to guard or keep their hearts? What are two or more ways you can make this practical in your life?

In Luke 6:45, Jesus contrasts a good man's actions with those of an evil man.

According to this verse, from where do our actions originate?

Proverbs 4:24–27 further teaches how to guard the heart. The heart and mouth are connected. Read Matthew 12:34 and Proverbs 4:24. The "froward mouth" of the KJV, and the "perversity" of the NIV mean *crookedness* or *deceitfulness*.

What are the instructions given in Proverbs 4:24? Are you often exposed to hearing this kind of talk? What can you do to obey the command to guard your heart?

According to Ephesians 4:29, what is the purpose of the believer's communication? List types of unwholesome talk that can be a temptation for believers (cutting others down, complaining, etc.).

Read Proverbs 4:25–27 and Proverbs 4:11–15. What instructions and warnings does the writer give about the paths referred to in these verses?

Are there distractions that cause your eyes and feet to stray from a level path? Note the commands in Proverbs 4:11–15. Write any verses or phrases that encourage you.

Meditate on Proverbs 3:5–7. Write each command contained in these verses. What is the result of such devotion to God?

Psalm 119:9–13 offers wisdom for guarding our hearts through diligently seeking God and his ways through the Word. Read these verses and write the phrases that call for acts of obedience.

Are you actively involved in these spiritual disciplines? In what way? If not, what is your plan to obey the Lord in these areas? What does the Psalmist ask God to do for him? Is this also a request you have of God?

Read Hebrews 4:12. What words indicate that the Word of God enters into the deepest recesses of our being? How is the Word helpful to the believer in guarding the heart or mind?

According to Luke 8:15, what is the process for developing a good heart? What is the result of having a good heart?

Why is it needful for the believer to persevere or be patient? The NIV's "persevering" and the KJV's "patience" refer to waiting with hopeful expectation. Do you desire to produce godly fruit from your life? Is guarding your heart a top priority?

Reflecting on your cross-cultural experience:

Has anything caused you to "fret" and feel anxious since your return?

What did you see or feel during your cross-cultural experience that caused you to fret or be anxious?

What changes during your absence were noteworthy or difficult for you to adjust to?

Are these experiences in your life turning you toward God with dependence upon his power and provision for you?

Prayer Suggestions:

Praise the Lord that he has given you his Word to penetrate and judge your heart. As you guard your heart, ask him to give you insight and discernment into that which you should avoid, and that which you can diligently apply. Thank the Lord for his forgiveness and cleansing that you can immediately receive through confession any moment that sin comes into your life. Pray about each command in Proverbs 3:5–7. Thank God for his promise to you of a productive, meaningful life if you guard your heart. Share your concerns and thoughts with the Lord. Ask him to help you understand and embrace the process you are going through.

(If you enjoyed this reentry devotional Bible study, check out www.DeeperRoots.com for information on the 14 day *Coming Home–Reentry Devotions For A Successful Return*, or *Coming Home Again–Reentry Devotions For Another Successful Return*.)

MINGLE
Matt Paschall, DELTA Ministries International

At midnight the mission team returned to the guesthouse gloriously exhausted. We had just witnessed the Spirit of God supernaturally move in the Serere village of Langomak in Senegal, West Africa. The chief, his three wives, and several adult men, women, and children made public professions of faith in Christ that night, forsaking the fear of the spirit world and bondage to the god of Islam. After two years of Christ-based health care, community development, literacy work, Jesus Film showings, and prayer teams from the national church leaders and missionaries, the ground had been cultivated and made ready—that night was the time for reaping. A new church was planted in the animistic-Muslim village in an unexpected, miraculous display of God's power.

When you spend six days a week for four weeks sharing your faith cross-culturally, it does something to radically change you. This mission team had worked hard alongside national pastors to share Christ with several villages. One adult team member, a manager of a car dealership in the States, told the team during debriefing about how this experience had changed him. "Now I feel convicted to share my faith more intentionally with those back at home." Focused times of evangelism during short-term mission projects often leave a common effect—reminding us of our life mission.

Whether you had anyone pray to receive Christ during your mission project or not, hopefully one thing that you took away from your short-term experience is that missions is not about something that we *do*. Rather, it is something that we *are*. We don't become missionaries by stepping onto a plane or traveling to another land. We are to always be on mission for God. Serving Christ and sharing his love is not about a program. It should be the driving passion in our lives. In the same way, evangelism is not something that we *do*. It is something that we *are*.

In Paul's charge to Timothy, he reminds him to maintain his mission passion and fulfill his work as an evangelist. "In the presence of God and of Christ Jesus, who will judge the living and the dead, and in view of his appearing and his kingdom, I give you this charge: Preach the Word; be prepared in season and out of season; correct, rebuke and encourage … do the work of an evangelist, discharge all the duties of your ministry" (2 Timothy 4:1–3 and 5).

As Christian evangelists, we should seek to follow the mandate, message, and model of our God who is always pursuing and reclaiming those who are lost in sin and rebellion against him. We should not wait until the next missions trip to share our faith, but instead be prepared at all times to give an answer for the hope that lies within us. Wherever the Lord has sent us to be a light, whether it is in the workplace, campus, family, community, or mission trip, we are to be on mission for God.

Evangelism is about building relationships with people for the purpose and glory of Jesus Christ. During the missions project, every effort, conversation, and encounter was motivated by a mindset of helping to bring others closer to the Creator. *Why do we lose this focus when we return home?*

We need to be intentional about mingling with others who need Christ. Rather than assaulting strangers around us with canned approaches or offensive tactics, we should supernaturally seek opportunities to speak about our relationship with Christ. Some people may not feel particularly gifted in sharing their faith, but the Great Commission was given to all believers, not just those with a supernatural gifting. God has given each of us an assignment and will ask us someday to give an account. Are you going to fulfill his purposes for his glory?

Extra Step: Identify two or three people that you will begin to pray for and share Christ with this week. Write a note, call, invite them over for a meal, or help meet a specific need. Then prayerfully seek opportunities to share with them the difference Christ has made in your life.

THE ENDURING POWER OF THE GOSPEL
Hans Finzel, WorldVenture

"We always pray for you, and we give thanks to God the Father of our Lord Jesus Christ, for we have heard that you trust in Christ Jesus and that you love all of God's people. You do this because you are looking forward to the joys of heaven — as you have been ever since you first heard the truth of the good news. *This same good news that came to you is going out all over the world. It is changing lives everywhere*, just as it changed yours that very first day you heard and understood the truth about God's great kindness to sinners."
Colossians 1:3–6 NLT

My father was one of the German rocket scientists involved with Dr. Werner Von Braun and the U.S. space program. My career has followed a very different course than my father's did. He helped build all of the rockets from the early Mercury program through Apollo, and eventually helped put a man on the moon in 1969.

I remember as a little boy growing up in Huntsville, Alabama when they test-fired the Saturn V rocket about fifteen miles from my house. The Saturn V is the rocket that sent the Apollo to the moon. It was bigger than the space shuttle and the largest rocket that the United States ever produced. When they test-fired the Saturn V, the windows in my house literally shook, and I thought we were having an Alabama earthquake! The awesome power of the Saturn rocket scared me as a little boy. It was the most powerful thing I had ever witnessed, much like Southern California earthquakes I actually experienced several decades later.

The gospel of Jesus Christ that we share has immeasurably greater power than the Saturn V rocket. I'm convinced that it is the most powerful force on earth. Why? It has the power to change people's hearts. Nothing is more challenging than to see people's lives changed, and nothing can do it but the power of Jesus. And the amazing thing about the gospel is that it has not lost any of its potency or power over the past 2000 years. Unlike batteries that lose their charge, the gospel is as hot today as it was in the early church. When Paul wrote Colossians, he said in verse six of chapter one, "This same good news that came to you is going out all over the world. *It is changing lives everywhere, just as it changed yours*." This verse is as true today as it was when Paul wrote that letter to the Colossian church. It is still changing lives everywhere it goes because of its incredible truth and power.

We missionaries are not the message; we are simply the messengers. We carry the greatest message that has ever been communicated on planet earth: the truth that Jesus Christ died for the sins of everybody throughout history. As we carry that powerful message, God can do his work as the truth reaches into human hearts. The most powerful thing I've ever witnessed in my life was not the test-firing of the Saturn rocket, but watching my own heart's transformation by the power of the gospel. The next best thing I've seen? Being a witness to others whose lives have also been changed as that message has been carried on.

Application Prayer: Thank you for changing my heart Lord Jesus. I am amazed that you want to use me to change others. Help me remember that I am just the messenger and that you are the one that changes people's hearts by the power of the gospel message. Use me, Lord, to carry this good news to those who, like the Colossians, are ready to receive it with joy.

MILE POST | 34

HOLE IN ONE!

Mary Alice Hughes with Felicity Burrow, International Mission Board (Southern Baptist Convention)

> "Be very careful, then, how you live—not as unwise but as wise, making the most of every opportunity, because the days are evil. Therefore do not be foolish, but understand what the Lord's will is." Ephesians 5:15–17

Raising money for student missions had never been as fun as it was the month when I "had" to play golf for the cause. It's a rough job, but someone had to do it, and I grudgingly (ahem) volunteered my services for the good of all student missionaries. My tournament partner, Mary Alice Hughes, won the longest drive contest for the tournament (she even beat the guys!), but I managed to hit a really good shot on one hole. Because of that one shot, I discovered a deep theological bent in Mary Alice. Here are her thoughts:

"Another highlight was my partner's hole-in-one! Yes, Felicity hit a hole-in-one on a beautiful par three. Unfortunately, she didn't see the ball drop in the hole. The ball hit the green, started rolling, and, being happy to see the ball on the green, Felicity bent down to pick up her tee...and missed the ball dropping into the cup! To prove that it really happened, Felicity walked up to the hole empty-handed and after looking in the cup, came up with a golf ball! I stood in awe, having never experienced playing with someone who hit a hole-in-one.

"I wonder how many times we miss great things that God wants to do in us and for us because we settle for 'hitting the green' instead of pressing on and expecting great things from him. For instance, as a student, how many times did I settle for a 'B' instead of pushing just a little harder for that 'A?' How many times have I just existed to get to tomorrow or through that next test instead of being aware of what God is doing around me so I can know him more? Or in work, how many times have I settled for 'just making it' instead of working harder to do my absolute best for the glory of God (1 Corinthians 10:31)?

"There was much celebration on that par three that day. Theresa, from our foursome, called and told everyone except President Bush, I think! But it's a shame that Felicity didn't get to see the completion of the great shot she hit. Let's learn from her hole-in-one and commit to keeping our eyes open for what God is doing all around us so we can celebrate a victory that we have seen and fully experienced. In other words, don't just settle for 'hitting the green.' Keep your head up and press on! Expect the best from God and don't be surprised when you get it!"

MILE POST | 35

ENTRUST
Terri Hughes Vincelette, CultureLink
Dottie Connor Bingham, Gracestoration

"For I know whom I have believed and am convinced that he is able to guard what I have entrusted to him for that day." 2 Timothy 1:12

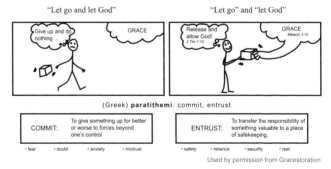

Used by permission from Gracestoration

You've heard the expression, "let go and let God." What does that mean? Maybe something really important is happening back home while you are on your mission trip. Or there is a team conflict going on that is affecting ministry and weighs heavy on you. Or you have met people who don't know Christ and you are deeply concerned about them after you leave. The most common advice for you is, "let go and let God" or "just commit it to God." Are you supposed to stop thinking or caring about it? Move on as if that issue or person wasn't a burden?

I don't believe that is what the Lord means when he asks us to trust him. The Lord knows how important burdens are to our hearts and lives. To just give them up is not within our ability.

The Greek word *paratithemi* is usually translated "commit or entrust." Commit means many things and can have positive or negative connotations. We commit in marriage and we commit adultery. We commit our lives to Christ and we commit murder in our hearts. *Commit* can mean "to give something up for better or worse to forces beyond one's control." What emotions usually follow when you just give up something valuable for better or for worse beyond your control? Look what's under the box on the left side of the picture: fear, doubt, anxiety, mistrust. We wonder if that person or issue is really going to be all right. We are unable to give up and do nothing.

> Everything is safe which we entrust to him and nothing is really safe which is not so entrusted.
> —A.W. Tozer

Now look at the right side of the picture. To "let go and let God" (trust God with something valuable) really means to "release and allow God!" 2 Timothy 1:12 assures us that we are able to do that. God is able to guard what we entrust to him. To entrust means to transfer the responsibility of something valuable to a place of safekeeping. It is like a safety deposit box. What kind of emotions follow entrust? Look what's under the box on the right side of the picture: safety, reliance, security, rest. The question is, "In your mind and heart, how safe is Jesus?" If you believe he is able to care for your burdens, then you are more likely to entrust those things to him.

We are to entrust ourselves (1 Peter 4:19), others (Acts 20:32), our ministry (Job 5:8), and our future (Psalm 37:4–5), and do it continually (1 Peter 2:23). The last thing the Lord Jesus did on earth was to entrust himself to the Father. "Into your hands I commit my spirit" (Luke 23:46). To continually entrust is to transfer the responsibility to Jesus *each time* a concern comes your way. He is able to keep and care for what we entrust to him.

> "Commit your way to the Lord trust in him, and he will do this." Psalm 37:5

MILE POST | 36

PEOPLE ONLY SEE WHAT THEY WANT TO SEE
Andy Spohrer, WorldVenture

"People only see what they want to see" is a statement often used to refer to a narrow way of looking at life and its events. But seeing life's events and opportunities accurately is critically important for a Christian, especially one who has a heart for God's glory to be spread over all the earth. How is your vision? What do you see as you look around you today?

In 2 Kings 6:8–17 we read the story of Elisha, his servant, and the whole town being surrounded by the Syrian army. Elisha's servant got up early in the morning and saw the enemy's armies and panicked. "Oh, my lord, what shall we do?" was his reaction. But Elisha could see much more, so he prayed and asked God to open his servant's eyes. His servant could then see what Elisha *knew* all along. He saw "the hills full of horses and chariots of fire all around Elisha!" Many of us have known Psalm 34:7 for a long time, "The angel of the Lord encamps around those who fear him, and he delivers them." But does this truth impact our immediate reaction to the crises that life throws at us when we feel surrounded by the enemy? Do we immediately see the horses and chariots of fire with God's angels, or do we panic with an "Oh, my lord, what shall we do?" I admit that I really want God to keep the enemy and all his problems *away* from me, but that is clearly not his plan. We *will* have trials and troubles in this life. My daily desire is to learn to trust God so much that I first see the horses and chariots of fire surrounding me rather than panicking. What do you see first when you encounter a problem?

How is your vision for the world? Jesus saw the multitude and was moved with compassion. Do you see the world today through the eyes of Jesus? Are you filled with compassion? Does that compassion have an impact upon your priorities and actions? Do you see the opportunities to "give a cup of water in Jesus' name" today? Sometimes we focus on the goal of our next mission trip or our move to longer term service overseas and we do not see the people right around us who so desperately need to know our savior. Perhaps it is someone who lives in your home or who works with you that God wants you to see. Perhaps it is the new neighbor who is an immigrant or the international students across town. How is your vision for the world?

How is your vision for the future? I am thinking of the long-range view. Jesus saw a day of rejoicing ahead of him so he endured the cross and pain of life here (Hebrews 12:2)! What do you see in eternity that encourages you today to endure life's troubles and to make appropriate sacrifices?

This is a good day for a vision check!

MILE POST | 37

RACIAL RECONCILIATION
David Jensen, Initiatives International

> "And there before me was a great multitude that no one could count, from every nation, tribe, people and language, standing before the throne and in front of the Lamb… And they cried out in a loud voice…" Revelation 7:9–10

My vision for short-term mission comes from this scene in the book of Revelation, where people from all over the world are before the Lamb's throne, busting out in the best multi-racial worship service that anyone could imagine! I get goose bumps every time I think about it. Can you feel the excitement, the passionate expression of that for which the human race was created? There is no better way to glorify God than when women and men of every ethnicity join together to offer themselves as living sacrifices before the great King.

I believe this passage not only describes a scene from our future, but also how we are to live, serve, and worship today. Many of you who have gone on a short-term mission have already experienced what I am talking about. You know the joy of joining your sisters and brothers in worship even if you don't understand their language. Many have told stories of being impacted by the experience of living, serving, and worshiping in another country or culture. These cross-cultural relationships have had life-changing effects on many who have gone, who have been hosts, and who have helped make the mission possible.

So why, then, does "the most segregated hour in America" still describe our Sunday morning worship? Curtis DeYoung and his co-authors argue in *United by Faith* that Christian churches, "when possible," should be multi-racial. We should intentionally be building multi-racial ministries that are welcoming and inviting to those of different ethnic backgrounds. What would your church look like if it were trying to be that kind of place? Perhaps the music would come from a variety of ethnic backgrounds. Perhaps there would be women and men of different ethnicities on the pastoral staff and in church leadership roles. Maybe the structure and decorations of the church would suggest a diverse body of believers. I'm sure we could find many ways to make our guests feel welcome if we set our creative minds to that task. What impact could we have? How would our lives be different?

Building multi-cultural relationships and churches requires cross-cultural skills and sensitivity, effort, and commitment. Most of all it requires grace, forgiveness, and humility. That is our calling and we must do what is right. This is a matter of justice, and the very reputation of God is at stake! It is not enough to enjoy brief multi-cultural moments during our short-term mission and then live out our lives in passive segregation. It is not enough to simply say that we are not personally holding prejudiced or racist attitudes. We must take what we have learned during STM experiences and commit ourselves to being reconcilers here at home. By building multi-racial relationships, we create a safe place for all to learn and grow in our understanding of each other. Those in the majority population must take responsibility for creating such places. If we as Christians cannot demonstrate that the love of God binds us all together across racial barriers, then how can we expect to be recognized as his disciples (John 13:34)?

MILE POST | 38

> "For we are God's workmanship, created in Christ Jesus to do good works, which God prepared in advance for us to do." Ephesians 2:10

I'm sure as you reflect on your short-term mission trip you can recall times when you needed to adjust your expectations and responses to various situations. During training events, some people's reaction to my teaching on the need to develop a flexible servant heart has been, "You're right; I need to adjust my expectations. You've done a good job in helping me prepare, but I'm sure everything will be all right on our trip." Looking back on their experience, however, they saw times when they had to make adjustments and realized the preparation had been essential.

I can remember just such a time when I thought I had it all under control, but God wanted to teach me a few things. I was with a team in Mexico ministering with a national church with whom we had worked for years. We rented a local swimming pool for an afternoon outreach with the church. It was a big deal for them to swim at this resort. I had made arrangements with the owners of the pool earlier in the week and had even paid a deposit. On the day of our outreach I arrived early with our team to get ready. I was shocked when we pulled up to the pool. I couldn't believe it ... the pool was empty and there were men cleaning it. Needless to say, I wasn't a happy camper. In talking with the owner he informed us that they always clean the pool on this particular day. Yet they didn't share that information when I made our reservation and paid the deposit!

I wish I could say I responded with the right attitude, but in fact, I was quite upset. The other team leaders handled it much better.

The owner said we could use the kiddy pool and have the place for free. As I pouted, the team got ready for the barbeque and began to play in the kiddy pool. A little while later, a national came up to me and asked what the problem was. I shared my disappointment in what I thought was to be an amazing day for all of us. He pointed out that if I would look at what was going on, I would see there were *more* people in the water because it was shallow. They were having a great time despite the circumstances. He then proceeded to throw me in the water!

The water checked my poor attitude, and I was reminded that from a kingdom perspective, what I thought was going to be a disaster, God intended for good (Romans 8:28). Things actually worked out better than I ever could have planned.

Now from the other side, I remind myself that life is full of the unexpected. Yes, at times it is not pleasant, and it may require adjustments, but God knows what is best. Experiencing adjustment to expectations can reveal a lot about us, whether we're just seeking our own desires or those of Christ. Developing the attitude that you desire God's best will not only help you process life's frustrations, but will enable you to even avoid those times by developing a heart like Jesus.

MILE POST | 39

PRAYING JESUS' WAY
Felicity Burrow, International Mission Board (Southern Baptist Convention)

Luke 10:2

It's crunch time. Your last papers are coming due, the presentation at work is just around the corner, the big project at the house is looming. You can, however, see the flicker of light at the end of the long, dark tunnel. Your plans—for work, school, or maybe missions—are beginning to gel. If you are going on a mission in the near future, you've probably begun asking friends and family members to pray for you and for the people you will serve. Jesus had a few tips for his followers about prayer and other things before he sent them out on a mission in Luke 10:1–16. These verses are basically a blow-by-blow account of the orientation class Jesus led for the 72 disciples who went.

In verses 4–9, Jesus tells his disciples not to worry about what they will wear or where they will stay. He also tells them to eat the food that is set before them. That advice is as practical today as it was in Jesus' day. Related to eating the food set before you, you could add the little "missionaries' prayer" that says, "Lord, I'll put it down if you'll keep it down."

Verse two is the one that captures my attention, though. In this verse, Jesus tells the disciples what to pray for as they go out on mission. My prayers tend to go something like this: "Lord, please prepare the hearts of the people with whom we will share so that they will be open and receive you as their Savior." Jesus didn't say anything like that though. He didn't say, "Ask God to touch the people's hearts so they will follow me." He simply said, "Ask God to send more workers."

My prayer was not a bad or wrong prayer, but it was not the kind that Jesus told his disciples to pray as they went to serve God. I want to pray the way Jesus asked his disciples to in Luke 10:2. This is only one of several ways Jesus taught his disciples to pray, but it is important. Jesus' priority in prayer is now at the top of my list of prayer priorities. As you go on mission, will you pray that God will send more workers to the place you go and the people you serve?

MILE POST | 40

HUMILITY
Bill Knepper, PastorShare, DELTA Ministries International

James 4:4–10

> "God opposes the proud but gives grace to the humble." James 4:6

Few verses in the Bible are more sobering than this one from James. We are told that God himself opposes or resists the one who is proud. That should make anyone very serious about understanding and practicing humility. So how can we learn to be humble?

We can teach ourselves humility by gaining a better understanding of the greatness of God. We are told that President Teddy Roosevelt had a practice of ending each day by standing on his balcony and gazing at the stars. He would say, "See that galaxy over there? It is larger than the Milky Way. It contains hundreds of billions of stars, all of which are larger than our sun." Then after a while he would say, "I think we are small enough now. It's time to go to bed."

We can teach ourselves humility by always honoring others rather than ourselves. Bear Bryant was one of America's all-time greatest college football coaches. Asked about his secret for building such strong teams, he said there were three things he would say. If anything goes bad, *I* did it. If anything goes semi-good, *we* did it. If anything goes real good, *you* did it.

We can teach ourselves humility by teaching ourselves to be silent. The story is told of the frog who wanted to hitchhike a ride south with the geese. The geese said there was no way they could carry him, so the frog came up with an idea. Two geese held a stick between their beaks and the frog held onto the stick with his mouth. It worked fine, too, until they flew over a farmer who said, "That's pretty clever. Who's idea was that?" "Mine," said the frog as he opened his mouth and fell to his death.

Our natural desire is to exalt ourselves and make sure we receive credit. But the Lord tells us that he, God himself, will come against the one who is proud. Strive to be humble because "God gives grace to the humble."

ATTITUDE
Andy Spohrer, WorldVenture

Attitude. That really says it all when you start thinking about where you have been on your mission trip and what you see now at your home church. It is unbelievable how insensitive Christians are toward the world's poor and suffering, isn't it? They waste money on all kinds of stuff from new, fancy cars to clothes to recreation to, well, you name it! And then they look you in the eye and say they don't have any money for your mission project! That really gripes me!!! You know what I mean? And they call themselves followers of Christ!

It is true that the American church, its people really, have material wealth that could change the world if it were channeled toward the world's suffering masses. Much has been written and discussed about this. But the issue for you today is your attitude toward your fellow Christians. How will you handle the discrepancy between what you have seen and experienced and how U.S. Christians use their wealth?

Jesus says a lot about not judging others and trusting that his servants will answer to him. But you and I must deal with our attitudes. In Hebrews 12:15 we are encouraged to do all we can to keep a bitter root from growing to cause trouble and defile many. Wow, that can happen so easily. We can be correct in our thinking but bitter in our attitude toward those who differ with us, and we end up causing trouble and seeing many defiled!

When we lived in Ireland, we rescued our back yard from the "millions" of stones that were there, and planted grass seed. Now, everyone knows that Ireland has 40 shades of green, so we were anxious to see those nice young grass shoots spreading over the lawn. And they came so nicely. But so did the big ugly weeds! And the weeds were bigger than the grass, so I decided to pull them up to get rid of them. Two unplanned results followed. Along with the ugly weeds, many young grass plants were pulled up by their roots. And some of the weeds had little prickly things on them that stuck into my fingers and hurt! Bitterness, according to Hebrews 12, takes root like the weeds in our lawn, and it is often the young, either people or grass plants, which are troubled or destroyed by it. And the person trying to get rid of the bitterness can also get hurt or defiled by doing so. Neither of these results honors God, nor will they get more people in our church committed to world evangelization!

You may have some correct ideas about the use of money or spiritual gifts for missions. But it is important that you hold your truth with the grace mentioned in Hebrews so that you do not get bitter and see people defiled rather than blessed!

MILE POST | 42

THE TYRANNY OF THE URGENT
Brian Stark, DELTA Ministries International

Luke 10:38–42

"Hello, my name is Brian and I am a workaholic!"

For me it started with a passion to do things and to do them well. I've always been a firm believer that what we do in representing Christ and proclaiming his name should be done with excellence because that is what the message deserves.

I also have an incredible desire to impact lives for eternity. There are so many ways to accomplish that—and so many needs. Let's face it, there are lots of good things out there worthy of my time and energy, and if I don't do it, who will?

As a vocational minister, I find myself filling my time doing lots of good things for God, forgetting that God really just wants me. Before I know it, days have gone by without any intimate communion with God

Jesus' interaction with Mary and Martha hits at my very core every time I am brought back to it. Martha is busy doing some very good things. Jesus and his entourage need to be cared for and looked after. They have been busy proclaiming the message of the kingdom and they need to be supported in that ministry in very practical ways. Mary, on the other hand, plops herself at Jesus feet, soaking up his every word.

I can sympathize with Martha. Why don't people get off their backsides and get busy with the ministry?! Yet Jesus shoots straight to the heart—beyond the actions to the attitude. He reminds each of us what God is truly after in his relationship with us. "Martha, Martha … you are worried and upset about many things, but only one thing is needed. Mary has chosen what is better, and it will not be taken away from her" (Luke 10:41–42).

God knows that I can do good things for him. He would rather I focus on the only thing necessary—knowing him and loving him above all else. The other stuff will come in time as a result of the knowledge and love I have for God.

As a workaholic, I can tell you the only way we can overcome this is to fall passionately in love with God. Watch and wait for him to lead, and then join him where he is working.

MILE POST | **43**

LOVING GOD WITH YOUR MIND
David Jensen, Initiatives International

"Love the Lord your God with all your heart
and with all your soul and with all your mind."
Matthew 22:37

The concept of loving God with all our heart and soul makes sense to most of us. Not that we have figured out how! But we have an idea of what we are talking about anyway. Loving God with our mind is different. How much time have we spent trying to figure out how to do that?

While there are several important applications, the purpose here is to consider the importance of education—developing your mind to its full potential. Now before you groan and turn the page let me suggest that this is an important part of being a Christ-follower. Your mind matters! Your ability to think critically and to communicate clearly has everything to do with how effectively you will be able to engage your world in the name of Jesus. Now that doesn't mean that we're all supposed to become university professors. Different gifts are given to each one. But it does mean that each person should develop the abilities that they have been given.

"To give less than 100 percent is to sacrifice the gift." The source of this quote was a t-shirt worn by a spectator at my son's track meet. Nevertheless it contains truth! God has given you some incredible gifts. One of those is your mind. If you do not take the development, discipline, and exercise of your mind seriously, then you risk wasting the gift that God gave you.

You have been stretched in ways you never thought possible on your short-term mission experience. You have learned many new things. Experience has been your teacher. Don't stop there. Now take what you have learned back to your life at home and continue learning. If you are a student, you have incredible opportunities to connect your STM experiences with what you are studying in school. Sometimes it may be hard to see the connections, but don't give up. Keep looking and you will find a deeper understanding of God and his world. If you've completed your formal education, continue on as a life-long learner. Reading, discussion groups, community education, and many more opportunities are out there for those still looking for ways to develop their minds. Look in your community for the people or groups who are addressing the issues that were brought to light while on your STM. Learn about what they are doing.

"Offer your bodies as living sacrifices, holy and pleasing to God" (Romans 12:1) definitely includes your mind. In fact, Romans 12:2 goes on to say, "be transformed by the renewing of your mind." It seems that there is no escaping the importance of developing your mind.

Having participated in a short-term mission, you are well on your way! Quality education must include a global, multicultural perspective. Look for study-abroad opportunities or ways to continue serving internationally. Jay Barnes, Provost of Bethel University, writes in an article called "Was Your Head with You Today?" that it is a mistake to stay on campus all the time during college. He encourages all students to take advantage of study-abroad opportunities. That is good advice.

So go on and learn something new. Don't waste the gift!

MILE POST | 44

THE PASSIONATE SEARCH
Matthew Harding, International Mission Board (Southern Baptist Convention)

"I love those who love me and those who diligently seek me will be found by me." Proverbs 8:17

My family and I love Chinese food. The word "love" may not even be adequate to describe our relationship with it. Some from afar may say that we are passionate about eating Chinese food. Not so long ago, my family and I were considering taking a trip back to our former college ministry to see some older students get married. Immediately my wife and I both felt that flash of passion. You could see the blaze in our eyes and the grins on our faces. Yes, we were not as excited about seeing old friends or former students as we were interested in hunting down our favorite Chinese restaurant in that town. We made the plans, packed the car, buckled the kids, and headed off five hours down the road with one end in sight— our favorite dish at our most favorite restaurant.

Well you can guess what happened. As we weaved in and out of traffic, drove at the speed of sound, zipped past all of our memories and friends, and excitedly bee-lined it to our gastronomical salvation, we learned all too quickly at the restaurant door that they were *closed*. Oh the pain and agony we felt (not really—but we sure did feel stupid and let down). The restaurant had closed for the holiday weekend and there would be no tasty morsels of Chinese delicacies on our lips.

Ah, but there is a poignant spiritual lesson here to learn, a huge "Jesus fortune cookie," if you will.

The world is full of sincere and desperate and even more passionate people on a great search for truth. They are moving head-long into a lifestyle of ritual and confusion as they think they have found the "right" way and the "perfect" solution to their needs. They move at the speed of sound in pursuing this faith that leads them ultimately to an eternally-closed door. As sad as it was to be rejected by a closed Chinese restaurant, my wife and I knew the spiritual parallel of life.

Many are seeking and even passionately *searching* for truth, for the one true God. Yet very few are committed to showing them the way. My wife and I could have made one simple phone call to make sure our Chinese venture would not have been in vain. Today millions are calling out, "Am I going the right way?" "Is the door closed at the end?" "Is there any way to know how to get to heaven?"

Are you committed today to be the one to go and share the truth that Jesus is the ever-open door for all who will find him? Cross your town and share his love with the people in the nearest Chinese restaurant and then go around the world to their back yard and point the way to the cross.

MILE POST | 45

EXPERIENCE THE JOY
Chris McDaniel, DELTA Ministries International

Psalm 40:5

2 Corinthians 8:8–12; 9:7

Recently published books indicate that there were overlooked early warning signs pointing to Enron's failure. The authors indicate out how individuals within Enron's leadership exhibited character flaws early in their careers. Warning signs such as previous risky and unethical financial practices, immaturity, and immoral behavior were present for all to see, yet many repeatedly missed the obvious.

How often do we miss the obvious in our lives? I believe the answer for many would be "all too often." Many times we fail to see how God blesses us each day. I've learned that taking inventory of God's blessings is the first step to not missing the obvious and gaining a greater appreciation for his love. Take a moment today to write down how God has blessed your life. Here are some questions to get started:

How has God blessed your family?

What friends has he provided in your life?

Do you have shelter, warm clothes, and food in your stomach?

How were you blessed from your short-term mission experience?

Do you have a job or source of income?

Do you have faith and a hope beyond this world?

Acknowledging how God has blessed helps us see how deeply he cares and is involved in our day-to-day lives. You will begin to remember and thank God for those obvious things that may have been overlooked in the past. Having our hearts in such a place allows us to give joyfully back to God, not out of obligation or compulsion. Counting your blessings is the first step to cheerful giving!

In 2 Corinthians 8:2 Paul states, "Out of the most severe trial, their overflowing joy and their extreme poverty welled up in rich generosity." The Macedonians faced no rest, harassment at every turn, outside conflict, internal fears, and poverty, but still, "urgently pleaded [to share] in this service to the saints." They were very aware of God's love and the blessings of the Gospel. The realization of blessings brought about generosity.

As we reflect upon all that God has blessed us with, may our hearts truly experience the joy of giving that God intends for us all.

Information taken from: **God and Your Stuff**, Wesley K. Willmer, Navpress, 2002

MILE POST | 46

GOD'S RENOWN
Suzanne Mosely, Director of Student Outreach at Union University

As I write this, I sit on my bed in a nice hotel in Bangkok, Thailand. Such a beautiful city with beautiful, gracious people! Despite the beauty surrounding me, my heart is deeply saddened by this place. Upon entering the local gas station, fast-food restaurant, or one of the hundreds of universities, the idol of each establishment can be found on display. My hotel has its idol proudly exhibited behind the front desk. Each idol has offerings of fresh fruit, money, and gorgeous flowers laid before its feet—offerings of appeasement with hopes for good fortune and blessing.

My mind quickly recalls Isaiah 26:8. "Yes, LORD, walking in the way of your laws, we wait for you; your name and renown are the desire of our hearts." My heart is saddened, yes, because the people are building their lives on a powerless idol who can offer them nothing. My true and primary sadness, however, is that God's name is not receiving the honor that he—and only he—deserves. His renown has not spread over Bangkok.

We sit in comfortable America idly watching our days pass. Is the name and renown of God truly the desire of our hearts? Do we lift prayers of intercession for the nations, tribes, and tongues who have never heard the truth of Jesus? Do our actions indicate that his name and his renown are the desires of our hearts? Are we grieved that God's name and renown is not known among 1.7 billion unreached peoples? These people are daily giving glory to other gods.

What gods in your life distract you from seeking God's re-

nown among the nations? Grades, a boyfriend/girlfriend, desire to be entertained, pursuit of money or power?

What can you do to shut the distractions out of your life? List two things you will do this month to focus on God receiving glory from the people groups of the world. Here are some ideas: pray for a people group using Matthew 9:37–38, befriend an international student at school, look in a Bible concordance for all the references to the "nations" and read those verses, write a praise song about taking God's love to the nations.

A heart enamored with God longs for him to receive the worship of members from every nation, tongue, and tribe. May the name and renown of God truly be the desire of your heart today. Such a life values spreading the name of the one true God above all else.

Lord, may all persons reading this today say with a pure heart, *"Above all else I desire your name and your renown."* May their lives be spent taking your name to the peoples of the world who are spending their lives making much of other gods.

MILE POST | 47

MAKE DISCIPLES, NOT DECISIONS
Hans Finzel, WorldVenture

> "Then Jesus came to them and said, "All authority in heaven and on earth has been given to me. Therefore go and make disciples of all nations, baptizing them in the name of the Father and of the Son and of the Holy Spirit, and teaching them to obey everything I have commanded you. And surely I am with you always, to the very end of the age." Matthew 28:18–20

Today's world is all about instant access and immediate results. No one wants to wait very long for anything. Thank God for the microwave! I get annoyed if more than one car is at the drive-up ATM. I am entitled to no waiting in line for my morning Starbucks! Is it any wonder that short-term missions is so popular? After all, can't we change the world by assaulting the mission fields of the world with short-term teams? There should be a quick fix for the world evangelism problem!

We are told that most Gen X'ers and Millennium kids will have seven careers. So who is thinking about spending a lifetime overseas on the mission field? This leads to the obvious questions, "Is there still a need for long-term missionaries? Can we get the Great Commission job done with short-term teams?" I think the answer is given plainly by Jesus when he gave us the Great Commission in Matthew 28:18–20.

Jesus instructed us to go into all the world and make something that would last. It was very clear that he did not ask us to *go and make decisions*, but to *go and make disciples*. There is a great difference in the two. And thus the difference in short-term and long-term missions. It's easy to go on a short-term mission and see decisions for Jesus Christ. It's meaningful to make short-term friendships with people of other lands. People can certainly make an immediate decision to follow Jesus, but that is not discipleship. It takes a long time to produce fully-devoted followers of Jesus Christ —what he called disciples. Like it or not, obedience to the Great Commission is a long-term process.

Short-term is great. But it takes the long view to make disciples. And what is so great about making disciples? Even if missionaries have to leave, the disciples will stay, grow, and reproduce themselves. We witnessed this in China over the decades in which all missionaries were thrown out and the church grew by millions because there were enough disciples left behind when the missionaries had to go. What's so great about disciples?

- They stick with the church.
- They last when we have to leave.
- They reproduce themselves.
- They create momentum and movements.

Never forget that the final and most important work of missions is the making of disciples. I am a big fan of short-term missions, but I know that it can only be a stimulus and a catalyst for those involved in long-term mission work. And without long-term missions there is no foundation upon which to build a short-term ministry. Short-term missions is real ministry, but we need to take the long view that it takes time to learn the culture and language of the people that Jesus wants us to disciple. Go into all the world and make disciples, not just decisions.

Application Prayer: Lord, help me to take the long view of the Great Commission. I love going on short-term mission trips, but open my eyes to your long-term plan for me. Use me to make disciples that will become fully devoted followers of Jesus Christ. If you want me to go for the long haul, show me the way and open the doors.

MILE POST | 48

GOING GLOCAL FOR GOD
John Dix, Grace Church of Glendora, California.

There is a new term that we have coined here at Grace Church. Actually, if you search google.com you'll find it, but it doesn't show up in a dictionary anywhere. It's the term *glocal*. I came home one afternoon and asked my seven-year-old daughter what two words she thought *glocal* came from. It took her about ten seconds to answer "global and local." That's it! The church is both local and global.

The church is local in reference to things like property, budget, programming, philosophy, staffing, and accountability. In fact, most every time the biblical term shows up in the New Testament it is referring to a local gathering of Christ-followers who are under the leadership of an appointed group of people. These churches are structured and organized around common goals, philosophy, and location. Even membership in these churches is implied from reading about them in Acts and the Epistles.

On the other hand Christ meant for the local church to be global in its reach and impact. "Go into *all* the world and preach the gospel to *all* creation" (Mark 16:15, emphasis added). God's vision for the church has always been, and always will be, international in scope.

When you talk to your neighbor about Christ or lend a helping hand to the needy, you are doing so as the church. When you get on a plane and go build a church building in Tanzania, you are doing it as the church. *You* are the church—local and global. We don't send groups from the church to do "missions" somewhere else. We are the church as we go … in Jerusalem, Judea, Samaria, and to the ends of the world. The church is glocal. You are meant to be glocal.

The distinction between local and global is lessening every year. The world is getting much smaller. When my grandparents left for Africa on October 26, 1929 they boarded a ship in New York harbor for a journey to Africa that would take them many weeks. Today I can get on a plane and be anywhere in the world within 24 hours. And more and more people of the world are coming to us. One year at Grace Church we focused our congregation on reaching our world right here at home. Our state hosts more international students than any other in the United States. That year alone we made a significant contact with at least one person from 148 of the 191 recognized countries in the world!

You are the church my friend—wherever you go, whatever you do, however you act, whenever you speak. What kind of "church" are you?

MILE POST 49

Matthew 26:6–13

> "Truly, I say to you, wherever this gospel is pro-claimed in the whole world, what she has done will also be told, in memory of her." Matthew 26:13

John tells us this woman was Mary, the sister of Martha and Lazarus. In fact, this story came shortly after Jesus raised Lazarus from the dead. It also came six days before the Passover, when the Messiah would be falsely accused and crucified.

Matthew, Mark, Luke, and John all record this tender moment. Our passage in Matthew only says the perfume was "very expensive." Others tell us it was worth an entire year's wage. (How much do you make in a year?) Yet, Mary broke the jar and poured it out on the feet of Jesus. She then wiped the excess off with her hair. Mary did not speak a word. The gospels tell us she wept as she poured out the perfume and wiped her Lord's feet. How much Mary understood about what was to come, we don't know. We only know that her act was a holy one because it was preparation of the sacrifice. It was a deed that honored the savior for what was about to happen.

Have you ever served someone at great expense to yourself and never spoken a word while doing it? Have you ever given deeply of what you have without being concerned whether anyone notices or even thanks you for it? Returning from the mission field, you can recall how much others have sacrificed to help you go. You remember those in other countries who carry on despite hardships. Coming home, you want to set the world on fire. Yet others will gladly grab the fire extinguisher and try to put you out!

Take some advice from Mary. Without a word she gave a great gift, served in a humble way, and honored her Lord. And Jesus said, "Wherever this gospel is proclaimed in the whole world, what she has done will also be told, in memory of her."

Start a ripple with those around you; don't just make waves.

MILE POST | 50

STAND IN THE GAP
Felicity Burrow, International Mission Board (Southern Baptist Convention)

Ezekiel 22:30

Interceding for the lost peoples of the world, including many completely unreached peoples like those in Indonesia or Saudi Arabia, is more familiar to people today than ever before. "Standing in the gap" is a phrase that has popularized prayer for the lost. Ironically, though, when God looked for someone to stand in the gap in Ezekiel 22, he was not searching for someone to intercede for the lost. Instead, God was seeking someone to intercede for the city of Jerusalem on behalf of God's own people who had fallen away from him.

In some ways, the American church is similar to the Israelites of Ezekiel's day — we have ignored the ways and purposes of God. Specifically, we tend to ignore God's global purpose for us to take the knowledge of him to all people groups on the earth. God clearly stated this plan five times in Genesis, beginning with Genesis 12:3. God said to Abram that he would bless Abram and all his descendents. They, in turn, would take the knowledge of God to all the nations on the earth. Many Christians today have camped on the blessing that God gives, but ignore the responsibility to take those blessings to all people groups on the earth so they will know about salvation from Jesus.

As you lift up prayer requests, stand in the gap also for the American church. Pray that American Christians will open their hearts to God's leading to reach the nations, whether that leading takes them around the world or down the street. You see, because we wouldn't go, God brought the nations to our country. Yet we still ignore them. Ask God how you can reach the nations around you and around the world. Pray that we will not be left behind as God accomplishes his global purpose, but that we will be an integral part of it. Stand in the gap on behalf of God's people to rise to the great global task God has given to us.

MILE POST | 51

FEEL THE BREEZE?
Andy Spohrer, WorldVenture

"Feel the breeze, Dad?" would occasionally be heard around our home when our daughters were teenagers. They would tell us about stuff from their day or about some topic of current interest and my face would show I had absolutely *no idea* what they were talking about. Their words were rushing right by me without stopping, so they figured I would "feel the breeze" but understand nothing. Often they were right! I was clueless. When I asked for more information, they would say, "Just forget it Dad. You wouldn't understand anyway."

Often when trying to convey to friends and fellow church members some of the experiences of a missions trip, I see that look in their eyes and want to say, "Feel the breeze?" because I know my words are flying right by them. My social skills, or more often my wife's knowing look, tell me it is time to shut up. So I do. But then I am tempted to be the one to "forget it" and move back into my comfortable life.

Jesus must have experienced some of these feelings in the Garden of Gethsemane. Matthew 26:36–46 tells the story of his disciples not understanding the urgency of the situation. They slept rather than praying and sharing his agony. "Could you men not keep watch with me for one hour?" (v. 40) indicates he wanted them to share his concern. But fortunately for us, Jesus did not "forget it" and move back into a comfortable life. He continued to spend time with his father in prayer and fellowship. He was strengthened by this time and was therefore able to face the cross for us. It was only later that his friends understood the significance of his agony and mission. Then they joined him, some even dying for his cause.

You have seen, smelled, touched, hugged, cried with and for, and shared your heart with people in a way that is truly impossible to convey to others in a few words or with a few pictures. But you have an idea what God wants *you* to do about your experience. You know he wants you to spend time with him—talking with him, sharing your heart and concern, listening to his heart for the people you met—and then responding as he directs. It may be that there are people from "your" country attending a university in your town. Maybe some have immigrated to your community. Perhaps you can connect with them for ministry and at the same time, keep your passion for the people alive. You can certainly keep contact with the others who traveled with you and who understand how it hurts when you sense people "feeling the breeze" from your words of concern. And email allows you to maintain regular contact with the people you worked with on the field. What a gift from God this is!

Some of your friends will understand your burden. Some will join you in prayer or in going back to help out. Yes, some may "feel the breeze," but as long as you do not "just forget it" God will strengthen you for the task he has for you as he did for Jesus in the garden!

MILE POST | 52

THE **BEST OR** YOUR **BEST?**
Brian Heerwagen, DELTA Ministries International

Colossians 3:17, 23–24

The little church framed by farmlands looked like a post card. Painted white, it had a sanctuary on the main floor and classrooms in the basement. Visitors from a summer short-term mission team would be joining this small congregation for services and VBS.

One of the team members had been asking to sing for a church service. The leader, knowing she couldn't sing well and lacked confidence, said that "maybe sometime" she could sing. But this was the last Sunday of the mission trip, and, in a moment of weakness, the leader said she could sing for this church.

There was no accompaniment, no starting note. Her eyes darted around the room as she sang. Her voice was shaky, and she was losing pitch, eventually singing monotone.

When the service ended, I made my way to the pastor to apologize for her poor performance before others could reach him. But I was too late. The woman in front of me cried as she told the pastor how she had not been to church for a long time and her life was a shambles. She felt compelled to come, and knew God had brought her to hear the angel who had sung that morning. She went on to say that the girl's crystal clear voice and the brilliance of her message was just what God used to touch her life. I was speechless. What had just happened? It was an embarrassing performance, yet the woman heard an *angel!*

And whatever you do, whether in word or deed, do it all in the name of the Lord Jesus. Whatever you do, work at it with all of your heart, as working for the Lord. This young lady had a song to sing and she did it as unto the Lord. So God blessed! To a perfectionist like me, it had been embarrassing. To God, it was a triumph!

Do you see the difference? Often we are consumed with what others think, or we're governed by our perfectionist tendencies, and we strive for *the* best. But God only asks for *your* best. The young girl could not perform to my standards, and she didn't try. She gave all she had from her heart. That is the gift God chose to use. He is blessed with an innocent and wholehearted offering to him, and he will use it to do things that our worldly best may never achieve.

We can still strive for excellence, but it must be as an act of worship only for the Father in heaven and not with the intent of impressing man. Do *your* best for him and let him take care of the rest!

Special Thanks

The Next Mile was made possible because of people like Daryl Nuss, Alex Areces, Chris McDaniel, Dianne Grudda, Shirley Radford, Asher and Pam Sarjent, Jeff Binney, Brian Stark, the entire DELTA Ministries staff, and the folks at Authentic Media. Thanks to all of you for your dreaming, studying, writing, and giving so much to this project.